# NOT,
# "JUST
# AN
# ADMIN!"

## DISCOVER THE RESPECT, VALUE AND POWER OF THE ADMINISTRATIVE PROFESSION

**If you've ever said or heard an admin say, "I'm just an admin," this book will change your view about the administrative profession.**

PEGGY VASQUEZ

Cover design and typesetting: Ambush Graphics

Library of Congress Control Number:  2014943366
ISBN # 978-0-9882307-5-0

1452 W. Horizon Ridge Parkway #555
Henderson, Nevada 89012
Published in the United States of America

# Table of Contents

# Foreward

This is a valuable handbook for anyone wanting to succeed. It is rare for us to find information that can make a difference both in our professional careers and personal relationships in one easy-to-read book. Filled with thoughtful questions and answers, this book leads the readers on an exciting and well laid out journey to understanding what it takes to achieve the success they desire.

A few years ago, I met Peggy Vasquez at an Administrative Professional Conference where I was the keynote speaker. I have watched her grow from a person who was nervous about introducing herself to me, into a confident, self-assured and highly successful professional. She has learned how to make things happen in her life and career and is passionate about sharing her knowledge with others.

There are many how-to and self-help books that tell you they can help you achieve success. You may have read many of them in an effort to improve the quality of your life and still feel there is more. This book is a personal journey with the author into self-discovery, self-respect, and self-confidence. Experience is a wise teacher. In writing this book and sharing her journey, Peggy supports and encourages you to find and achieve your dreams. She is committed to her purpose – helping others succeed. With an unabashed passion for her profession, she encourages, mentors, and empowers others. While this book is geared to the Administrative Professional, I see it as worthwhile reading for anyone in the corporate world.

**JUDI MOREO, AUTHOR**
YOU ARE MORE THAN ENOUGH
ACHIEVEMENT JOURNAL

# Respect:
# You've Got To Give It To Get It

"Self-respect cannot be hunted.
It cannot be purchased.
It is never for sale.
It cannot be fabricated out of public relations.
It comes to us when we are alone,
in quiet moments,
in quiet places,
when we suddenly realize that,
knowing the good, we have done it;
knowing the beautiful, we have served it;
knowing the truth, we have spoken it."

**–WHITNEY GRISWOLD**

CHAPTER**ONE**

# Respect:
# You've Got To
# Give It To Get It

**T**error! That's what I felt the first time I was asked to give a presentation at an upcoming conference. Instead of feeling excited about the opportunity as I had in the past. I had a huge feeling of heaviness about the whole thing. I had a new sense of responsibility to answer the "cry for help" I had been hearing. Over the past several months, the same conversation kept being repeated, almost as if someone was playing the same song over and over again and as each word is sung you know what the next lyric is going to be. It was becoming a Déjà vu type of experience. The "cry for help," message I was hearing and am still hearing is: "People don't respect me and my role as an administrative assistant. I don't feel valued. I don't feel respected." I realized that my terror stemmed from my own feelings that others did not respect or understand the position I was in and what it actually entails. I am not JUST an admin!

When I first heard the message, it felt like someone was having a bad day or on a train ride to "Victimville." Over time, the message started sinking in and I realized the "value and respect" message was a real issue to many administrative assistants. (*I believe this feeling is becoming more and more prevalent for anyone in the work force today, not only for the administrative professional career family.*) I realized the "cry for help" wasn't just someone whining or being a victim. It was a deep seeded pain and a feeling difficult to admit or express. Those sharing the message were not just venting…they wanted change! They wanted the situation to shift and didn't know what to do to cause a change. What made it worse for me was I didn't have an answer. All I could do was listen to their pain and frustration with compassion. I left each interaction feeling frustrated. The energy to solve the problem was swelling up inside of me and the desire to provide an answer was growing.

Then one day the answer came to me, seemingly out of the blue. (*If you're anything like me, this happens often and we both know it is a gift, like manna from heaven, right?*)

Here's what I heard:


The answer is

It all begins with us, as individuals and

administrative professionals! First and most

importantly, we must have self-respect.

Secondly, we must have respect for

our profession as administrative assistants,

and, lastly, we must demonstrate

respect to others.

It's a "**Got to Give It to Get it**" response. We must have self-respect and respect our profession. Then, actively demonstrate respect for others. When we act in this manner, we greatly shift the way others treat us. Our actions cause a reaction. When we respect ourselves, others treat us respectfully.

I've worked for many different executives over the past thirty years. About six months after accepting one position, I learned that my manager had a long history of being disrespectful to his former assistants. Thankfully, no one shared this news with me in the beginning. If they had, I likely would have believed he was a horrible manager and would have brought negative energy and behavior to the relationship which would have created an entirely different dynamic. Instead, I believed this was a great opportunity and brought all my best skills and positive attitude to the new position. In fact, when I learned about his poor reputation, I was completely surprised because what was being described had not been my experience at all. I believe this was largely attributed to the dynamic we created together.

When you begin a new partnership, each person brings his or her own dynamic to a situation, including past experiences, baggage, self-respect or lack of respect and many other aspects. All of those attributes create the unique dynamic between the people involved. It is the essence we bring to a situation that causes people to treat us in a certain manner. The way in which a manager may have treated a former assistant doesn't mean it is the way he or she will treat you. We all have the ability to shift our thinking and our behavior. *(We'll talk more about partnerships later.)*

So, how do we make the mental shift? Where do we start? We begin by having healthy self-respect and valuing ourselves.

## SELF-RESPECT

If you want to be respected by others, you must respect yourself. Only then will others feel compelled to respect you.

We are much more than our administrative assistant role. Most of us have many different roles as well: spouse, sibling, friend, parent, grandparent, to name a few. We are individuals with values, principles, interests, strengths, talents, goals and dreams. The latter is what truly defines us and makes us much more unique than any role we chose to play.

Our greatest moments are when we are in the service of another. Experiencing numerous leadership retreats, attending and speaking at several administrative conferences, and reading a multitude of self-help books, all pointed me to this belief. Motivational speaker, Zig Ziglar, sums it up really well: "True joy comes when you inspire, encourage, and guide someone else on a path that benefits him or her."

During a leadership team retreat, the teams were given the assignment to write our personal mission statements. The consultant limited us to one short sentence. Most of us began with a long paragraph and it took several passes to condense our wording to the required one sentence assignment. Some of the team members wrote flowery and beautiful mission statements, other team members mission statements were bulleted statements. When we had completed the assignment, each team member's mission statement was clear and easy to understand. The one I wrote over twenty years ago is still my same mission statement today:

# Peggy's Mission Statement:
# "I empower others to succeed."

Have you ever noticed the feelings you have when you are helping someone else? Why would we rather help one of our friends clean her home instead of doing our own dirty dishes? Why is it more fun to organize someone's office instead of our own piled up workspace? It makes us feel good! When we serve others, we are filled with positive feelings. We know we have helped someone and he or she is better because of our actions. We have a sense of accomplishment and purpose. We know our act of kindness, no matter how small or how large, has created a ripple effect on that person's life and, therefore, on other lives!

# Life is good when we know the world is a better place because we have lived.

## VALUES

Knowing your values and living by them enables you to experience self-respect. Your values are engrained in your heart, mind, and soul. Your values are your guiding compass and will steer you forward. Your values are what you access to make tough decisions. Your values help you stay on course when things are difficult.

There are many exercises available to discover your values. If you haven't done an exercise before or if it's been awhile, I encourage you to take a moment to discover, or to rediscover your values. The following is an abridged version of the one I teach in my "Be True To You" class.

There are six main areas of your life: Health, Relationships, Lifestyle, Career, Spirit and Wealth. As you consider these facets of your life, ask yourself, "What would make me happy in each one of these areas?" Write down the first two to three things that pop into your mind for each area of your life below. There is no right or wrong answer. These are your answers. These identify what you value, want, and desire.

Pause for just a moment and imagine you are at your annual doctor's appointment and you have just heard your doctor say you have an inoperable disease and have 12 months to live! Take a moment to really let that feeling and the emotion sink in. What if 12 months was all the time you had left on this earth? What would become most important to you? What would rise to the top of your list of desired experiences? Where would you want to spend the most time? On what would you focus?

Typically, after going through this experience, we need to reassess what we originally wrote down and what we thought we wanted in each of the six areas of our lives. Do your initial responses regarding what would make you happy still have relevance and meaning? Does it make sense? Is it a priority? Or, do you need to make new choices?

There was a time in my life when I was completely out of balance. By the way, I believe "life balance" is a myth! I don't believe anyone spends proportionate times in each of the six areas of his or her life day after day! If you believe that is what you need to do in order to be balanced, you are setting yourself up for a huge disappointment. The reality is, at times your focus may be more on family due to raising small children, other times it may be on your career due to a recent change of employer, or it may be on your health due to a recent trip to the doctor! Your life becomes that on which you spend your time and where you focus. If your focus is only on one area of your life for a prolonged period of time, you are likely way out of balance. I experienced one of those prolonged periods of time and almost all of my focus was on wealth and my career. My husband and friends can tell you, it was all I ever did or talked about! My focus, my time and my thoughts weren't about my health, my family, or my spirit. My entire focus was on my career and wealth.

One day, I was sitting in a doctor's office for my annual appointment, watching the clock and growing more and more frustrated as an hour passed by and I no longer had anything to "work" on. This was long before smartphones, laptops and iPads. The only thing left to do was to look through the magazines in the waiting room. To my disappointment, the only ones they had were "women's" magazines. You know the types: *Redbook, Parents, Home and Garden*, the soft and mushy types, not the career and money hungry type of spreads I was interested in reading. Well,

I was bored to the point that I started thumbing through these women's magazines and was soon submerged in articles about women's health, family, home and relationships. I was so NOT interested. I couldn't bring myself to read one article. I thumbed through page after page looking for something relating more to careers when suddenly I came across a picture of a tombstone and the headline read,

# What will be engraved on your tombstone?

I'll never forget that moment. It hit me so hard, as if the tombstone had sprung off the page and hit me across my head! What had happened to me? How did I get so far off track? I didn't want what I was chasing to be written on my tombstone. Who writes, "Amazing Employee" on her tombstone? What I wanted engraved was, "Amazing Wife and Mother," however I wasn't being an amazing wife and mother. I was selfish, self-centered, and focused only on me and my career. I hadn't realized how far away I had drifted from my core foundational values until that moment. It was a tremendous wakeup call.

I am forever thankful for that doctor running two hours behind schedule. She doesn't even know it, but she saved my life by putting those magazines in her waiting room. I had the good fortune of receiving a wakeup call before I was on my death bed full of regret and wishing I still had 12 months left to live a life according to my values. I had the chance to get my life back on track. That one moment made me re-think everything.

As you look at what you wrote in each of the six areas of your life and you find what you originally wrote doesn't align to your values, it's time to re-assess and re-focus on the things that really matter the most to you. This is what it means to be "true" to you...to live by your values. Doing so will provide you with tremendous self-respect and genuine happiness.

We earn self-respect, when we live according to our values. When we do the things that are aligned to our values, we are demonstrating self-respect. When we listen to our inner voices and say the things out loud that are in our hearts and minds and when we passionately feel we must voice our thoughts and feelings, even when they are difficult and unpopular, we earn self-respect. Honoring our values and acting upon those beliefs in the face of adversity or risking approval of others can be difficult and is exactly what is needed to obtain self-respect. It is when we disregard our values and our inner voices that our self-respect erodes and we begin to act "less than." Self-respect is knowing we are not less than others...instead we are equal. We are good enough to deserve love, happiness and success. We are good enough to be treated with respect from others and, most importantly, from ourselves.

> "Respect yourself
> and others will respect you."
>
> **–CONFUCIUS**

Self-respect is not thinking we are better than someone or having a large ego. It's keeping a healthy balance based on our values and being aware of our short comings and our accomplishments. It's having and showing respect to others.

## RESPECT FOR OUR ROLES

When was the last time you really thought about what was in the palm of your hand as an administrative assistant? As assistants, we have tremendous power to influence our managers and others around us. We often act as advisors, counselors, coaches and mentors. We also act on behalf of our managers.

As I think about the many executives I've supported, I can easily recall moments where only my executive and I knew about a particular situation. He trusted me implicitly and needed someone to confide in. Behind closed doors, we discussed the situation and all the nuances. We weighed out possible options. Together, we strategized and determined the next steps. It's in these moments that our role is extremely valued and we, as individuals, are held in the highest regard. When your executive knows you are there to make him or her and the company successful; you are treasured more than any recognition ceremony could possibly indicate. These are the moments I cherish. These are also the moments of power and, if used respectfully, we can make a positive difference. Administrative assistant's shape and influence business decisions. Honor and respect your role. Use it for the greater good.

Over time, you will see how you directly made a difference as you hear your executive repeating words you provided, using your ideas for a new approach, and implementing decisions you made together as business partners.

There are only a few positions with this type of power and influence and being an administrative assistant is one of them!

We also have confidential information we share based on business protocol and sound judgment. There are times we learn about information we wish we didn't know, especially in times of mergers, organizational restructures, budget shortfalls, downsizing, legal issues, poor performance consequences and resignations. These situations are all calls to leadership. It is imperative that we hold this information in the utmost of confidence, even when it may directly impact those we are close to and care about.

When going through a large restructure, one of my closest friends disagreed with the approach the leadership team had implemented. She came to me full of energy, doubt, fear, and anger over the plan to change her organization and the team structure. Fortunately, I had been involved in the meetings where the discussion and decisions were made. Without disclosing confidential information, I was able to give her enough insight to help her shift to getting on board. What really helped her move forward was when I told her the leadership team didn't make a quick decision, that all possibilities were considered and on the table for discussion, even the ones she had just shared with me. It also made a significant impact that I genuinely cared and listened to her concerns. These are the moments when we act as change agents to carry out the decisions of our executives. *Again, administrative assistants have tremendous influence and power…* Power that can be used to make a positive difference in the lives of those we work with and support.

Given this same situation, what would the outcome have been if I would have sided with my friend? What if I had joined in on the negative spin, found fault with the leadership team's decisions, talked about all that was wrong with the restructure, and asked questions that produced seeds of doubt? If I would have pointed my finger at the leadership team and said that I didn't agree with their decision, but it's what "they" decided, it would have had a negative impact. When you are part of a powerful partnership, you must be part of the team. You can no longer point to "they" because you are part of that team. Think about how you've used your power and influence in a positive or negative way.

We've all heard the phrase "actions speak louder than words." Our words and actions need to demonstrate respect for others and for ourselves. Doing what we say we'll do and being trustworthy shows our character. By demonstrating self-respect and respect for others, we'll earn and keep respect.

When we respect ourselves, it shows and encourages others to treat us respectfully. When we don't respect ourselves and our positions, we might as well put that message up on a billboard for everyone to read because it's that obvious! When we act disrespectful of ourselves or our position, others will most likely treat us disrespectfully.

## CALL TO ACTION!

If you find yourself saying or believing: "People don't respect me and my role as an administrative assistant. I don't feel valued. I don't feel respected." Then it's time to take action and be part of the change.

### I Challenge You to Take A Stand and Join Me:

1. Be one of the best administrative assistants you can imagine.

2. Demonstrate self-respect.

3. Demonstrate respect for the administrative profession.

4. Show respect to others.

5. Share this message with others; ask them to join you in this challenge.

Shifting a culture and eliminating stereo types takes concerted effort, time and patience. Raising the respect for the administrative profession won't happen overnight. It won't happen if only one or two of us demonstrate these behaviors. Individually, we can make a difference for ourselves. To make a difference for the administrative profession as a whole takes all of us taking on this challenge. Imagine for a moment that every administrative assistant you knew demonstrated these behaviors!

Together,
we can make a difference!
It begins with us, as individuals
and administrative professionals!
First, and most importantly,
we must have self-respect.
Second, we must have
respect for our profession
as administrative assistants,
and, lastly, we must
demonstrate respect to others.

# Your Image is You!

"Your presence makes a statement about you.

What does your presence say?"

CHAPTER**TWO**

# Your Image Is You!

Image is much more than simply the clothes on your back. It is your entire package. It's the way you look, talk and act. It's your character. It's what you stand for and believe in. It's the messages you communicate. It's your wardrobe and the way you wear it. It's your style. It's your personal expression. It's your uniqueness. It's what people remember about you. It's your brand! Your image is you!

When was the last time you looked in the mirror and asked yourself, "What is my image? What does my reflection tell me?"

## Embracing your image begins with embracing the mirror!

Let's begin with our physical image. Most of us aren't confident about our bodies. We question how we look, our weight, and our shapes. We judge our fashion choices, our hair, and even our makeup.

Last year, the fashion industry employed 4,200,000 people and had revenue of $1,200,000,000,000! That's a lot of people and dollars telling us how we need to look and what we need to wear in order to feel and look fabulous! In case these figures didn't get your attention, here's a few more. According to research by Harry

Beckwith, in 5–10 seconds, we judge each other's physical image and make 11 major decisions about each other!

The reality is people judge how we look, what we wear and how we carry ourselves. To be successful, we need to learn what to do and what not to do to make sure our image is judged in the most positive light possible.

Your appearance makes a statement about you…from your hair, to your clothes, to your shoes, to your handbag and eyeglasses. Your "wrapping" tells others how you feel about yourself. It gives the message that you care enough to take care of yourself, or it can tell people that you don't care about yourself and you do not invest time or money in yourself.

Your presence is your 'present.'

People identify your success according to your 'wrapping.'

You are a gift, so present yourself impeccably wrapped!

I've always loved fashion. I love looking at the new designs and colors for each season as well as looking at vintage designs. Due to my fashion interest, paying attention to my image wasn't difficult or a stretch for me. It was a way to express myself. It's somewhat of an art to mix and match patterns and shapes to create the illusion you want to portray. I paid attention to the latest fashions and the way people dressed where I worked. I paid the most attention to the people I respected, were successful, and held the types of position I wanted. I knew if I were to have what they had, I needed to emulate them in the way they dressed, how they interacted with others, and the attitude they expressed.

One of the former companies for which I worked had a dress code that was heavily enforced. This was the first and only company I worked for in my thirty year career that had a dress code. Whenever someone talks about a dress code, it usually brings up a lot of intense emotion and argument. Everyone has an opinion and has a reason why an exception should be made.

Interestingly, most of the aspects from that first dress code are still embraced or bring up controversy today.

1. No open toed shoes

2. No sling back shoes

3. No sleeveless clothing

4. No jeans

5. No T-shirts

6. No bare legs, hose required

Some of you may cringe when you read through these rules. Some of you may love them and wish every company reinforced rules such as these. Some of you may want to argue and say these are old fashioned rules and don't apply today.

I've learned there is a great deal of emotion over dress codes and to treat this topic respectfully and carefully. This chapter is not about rules, or who is right and who is wrong. Instead, I simply want to share with you what I've learned and observed, what works and what doesn't, as well as how you can follow these guidelines and still express your individuality in a way that honors you and your company.

Years ago, at a former company, I was given the role of dress code enforcer and had the "opportunity" to learn firsthand how difficult this role can be! I thought it would be pretty straight forward. Boy, was I naive! One co-worker just didn't get it. We talked about the dress code and what was acceptable and what wasn't. I thought we had an understanding and an agreement and, yet, she would show up to the office dressed in pony print pants, a crop top showing her stomach, and strappy platform shoes with 6 inch heels!

# What are you selling?

I was at my wits end trying to get through to her. I kept thinking, "How can I explain the dress code to her in a way that she gets it and understands the bigger picture?" I wanted her to understand how following this standard could help her become more successful. I knew focusing on "rules" she needed to follow wasn't the answer. Then, it finally hit me. I needed to meet her where she was in life and not from where I was. I needed to remember that not everyone had the same interests and shared observations as I had on my career path.

I approached her in private. I complimented her pony pants (they really were cute, even if they were completely out of place). We chatted for a few minutes. Then, I asked her if she was going out after work. She responded she was as it was Friday. I asked if she was going home to change first. She said no, with a furrowed brow and inquisitive look on her face. Then I said, "That is exactly why you shouldn't wear this outfit to work no matter how cute it is or how great you look."

# If you can wear your outfit from work to the club, it's not the right outfit to wear to work.

She finally got it! I never had to talk to her again about the company dress code. I was honest with her and talked to her in a gentle, yet firm manner. I let her know I cared about her and wanted to help her be successful. I explained if she wanted to be taken seriously at work, she needed to dress and act the part. The best part about the conversation was it opened the door for continued mentoring.

## BUILDING YOUR CLASSIC WARDROBE

When I first began my career I didn't have the same resources I have today. However, I wasn't about to let that stop me from looking the way I wanted to look. I got creative. I employed my resourcefulness and began shopping at vintage stores, consignment shops and a variety of second hand stores. It was fun shopping to see what treasures I could find. You'd be surprised if I told you how long I continued to frequent these types of shops. I have been complimented on my wardrobe for years and there were times my entire outfit cost less than $10.00! You don't need to spend a fortune on clothes in order to be dressed successfully. You just need to know what works for you based on your style, your coloring, and your body type.

**Women:**

My advice for women is to invest in four well-fitting classic pieces: A jacket, trouser, skirt and dress. Your next investments should be a neutral blouse and a colorful scarf, which can quickly create a fresh new look to your classic suit, a large handbag that can double as a briefcase, and a small purse for your personal belongings.

**What doesn't work:**

Avoid wearing anything you would wear to wash your car or wear to the beach. Avoid wearing anything you would wear out to a club or cocktail party.

**Men:**

My advice for men is to invest in a two piece suit in a neutral solid gray or navy. If your suit jacket and pants are solid instead of a print, you'll be able to wear them easily with other pieces. Choose your ties carefully. When in doubt, it is best to lean towards a conservative look, something that adds a pop of color, and, yet, others don't notice it before they notice you.

Nothing will look cheaper than a pair of shabby shoes with a nice suit. You can get by with one pair of shoes as long as they are in good shape and freshly polished.

Avoid wearing a backpack as it will immediately give off a juvenile vibe and give an impression of too young for the business world. If you don't have a briefcase or a messenger bag, make one of these your next investment.

## INVEST IN THE CLASSICS

You can never go wrong with the classics. Every business man and woman should have at least one well-fitting grey, black, or navy suit and a crisp white shirt in their wardrobe. Select jewelry, scarves, ties, and shoes to express your unique sense of style. This is where you can get creative and show your personality. You can take a conservative navy suit, put on a colorful bold patterned scarf and still look sharp and professional. You can wear a great fitting pair of trousers with a buttoned up shirt, polished shoes, and some accessories and look ready for business as well.

# CLASSIC CAREER WARDROBE ESSENTIALS FOR WOMEN

| Dresses & Skirt | | Pants | | Tops | |
|---|---|---|---|---|---|
| Little Black Dress | | Black Trousers | | Dressy Tank | |
| Feminine Day Dress | | Khaki Trousers | | Silk Camisole | |
| Long-Sleeve Knit Dress | | Grey Trousers | | Simple Black Tee | |
| Shirt Dress | | Black Cigarette Pant | | Simple White Tee | |
| A-Line Skirt | | Regular Jeans | | Polo Shirt | |
| Black Pencil Skirt | | Skinny Jean | | Striped Boat neck | |
| Grey Pencil Skirt | | | | White Cotton Button Up | |
| Navy Pencil Skirt | | **Footwear** | | Silk Blouse | |
| | | Black Ballet Flats | | Tunic | |
| | | Loafers | | A few Classic Sweaters | |
| | | Sneakers | | Short Cardigan | |
| | | Black Sandals | | Long Wrap Cardigan | |
| | | Tan Sandals | | | |
| | | Black Pumps | | | |
| | | Natural Colored Heels | | | |
| | | Colorful Heels | | | |
| | | Tall Brown Boots | | **Accessories** | |
| | | Tall Black Boots | | Shawl | |
| | | | | Silk Scarf | |
| | | | | Neutral Leather Handbag | |
| **Bling & Baubles** | | | | Evening Clutch | |
| Diamond Studs | | | | Casual Tote Bag | |
| Pearl Studs | | | | Colorful Skinny Belt | |
| Pearl Necklace | | | | Tan or Black Skinny Belt | |
| Gold Dangles | | | | Wide Brown Waist Belt | |
| Silver Dangles | | | | Wide Black Waist Belt | |
| Pendant Necklace | | **Outerwear** | | Opaque Tights | |
| Gold Ring | | Trench Coat | | Black Bikini | |
| Silver Ring | | Wool Coat | | One Piece Swimsuit | |
| Understated Watch | | Lightweight Jacket | | Tortoise Shell Sunglasses | |
| Oversized Watch | | Navy Blazer | | Straw Hat | |
| Simple Bracelet | | Black Blazer | | Floppy Hat | |
| Dressy Bracelet | | Denim Jacket | | Umbrella | |

# CLASSIC CAREER WARDROBE ESSENTIALS FOR MEN

| Suits | | Tops | | Pants | |
|---|---|---|---|---|---|
| Navy Blue Suit | | Cotton Polo | | Jeans | |
| Charcoal Grey Suit | | Long Sleeve Polo | | Khaki Chinos | |
| Light Cotton Suit | | Cotton Oxford | | Navy Chinos | |
| Tuxedo | | Gingham Oxford | | Charcoal Trousers | |
| | | White Dress Shirt | | Black Trousers | |
| | | Light Blue Dress Shirt | | Navy Trousers | |
| | | Crewneck Sweater | | | |
| | | V-Neck Sweater | | | |
| | | Classic T-Shirt | | | |
| | | Vest | | | |

| Accessories | | | | Ties | |
|---|---|---|---|---|---|
| Simple Cuff Links | | | | Black Bow Tie | |
| Tie Clip | | | | Striped Tie | |
| Money Clip | | | | Solid Tie | |
| Card Holder | | | | Club Tie | |
| Signet Ring | | Shorts | | Trendy Bow Tie | |
| Casual Watch | | Khaki Shorts | | Bright Pocket Square | |
| Dressy Watch | | Navy Shorts | | | |
| Leather Wallet | | Dark Khaki | | | |
| Black Leather Belt | | | | Footwear | |
| Blown Leather Belt | | | | Basic Sneakers | |
| Dress Socks | | Outerwear | | Loafers | |
| Bright or Stripe Sock | | Trench Coat | | Boots | |
| Leather Briefcase | | Navy Blazer | | Black Dress Shoes | |
| Canvas Weekender Bag | | Leather Jacket | | Brown Dress Shoes | |
| Printed Swim Trunks | | Peacoat | | Boat Shoes | |
| Sunglasses | | Tweed Sport Coat | | | |
| Scarf | | | | | |
| Umbrella | | | | | |

## DO NOT DISCOUNT THE IMPORTANCE OF FIT

One of the most important aspects of clothing is fit! I am 5'4" which is on the cusp of a petite. It is extremely rare that I can buy and wear clothing off the rack. Most of the time, I have to get my pants and jackets altered. A jacket, no matter how expensive, isn't worth wearing if it doesn't fit in the shoulders, sleeves, waist and length. Tailoring is essential. Whether your tailor is your mother, the dry cleaners, or a professional – find one!

Most men's suits come un-hemmed and altering is often included in the price. Men's shirts come in neck and sleeve sizes. This is not the case for women; therefore, women need to invest in tailoring. Think of it this way, the clothing manufacturer didn't make a line for you or for me, but a tailor can. There's nothing that speaks success louder than a well-tailored suit. You and your image are worth the investment.

## BODY SHAPE

Each of us was born with a unique body shape, not a right or wrong shape, just a unique shape. The number on the scale isn't right or wrong. It is simply a measure of where we are at this moment in time. The key is to learn about our own unique shapes and learn the secrets to highlighting our best assets. Learning about our body shapes is critical to our success in dressing to make us look and feel fabulous.

A woman's goal is to make her body shape look like an hourglass. Whether you are a triangle, diamond, rectangle or the coveted hourglass, you can use patterns, colors, and styles to create the illusion desired.

You can determine your shape by asking a friend or your tailor to measure you or simply by trying on different styles to determine what works best for you. My advice is to not get hung up on your shape, but instead, invest time in the dressing room. Try on a variety of styles and colors. Find out what works for you and makes you feel the most confident. Ask a friend to join you and to provide honest feedback about what styles provide you the most flattering shape.

You'll want to try on a variety of styles, colors, shapes and patterns. Take your time in the dressing room. Find out what necklines look best on you. Do you look best in an A-line dress or a pencil skirt? Determine if belts are complimentary for your shape or if a drop waist is more flattering. Consider what style or color you are wearing when you receive the most compliments. If you have gorgeous legs, show them off with a great skirt or dress. A well-tailored jacket that flatters your waist line can be your best friend. Experiment, have fun, and be open to the process.

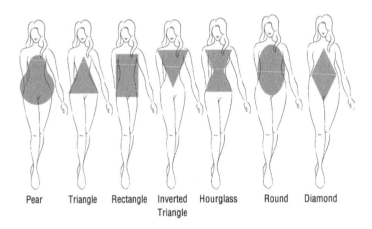

Pear    Triangle    Rectangle    Inverted Triangle    Hourglass    Round    Diamond

While in the dressing room, do the "Sit and Lean" test. Sit down to determine if the garment still fits comfortably? You may notice, when seated the skirt rides too high or is too tight. Lean forward. Does the neckline gap and show too much cleavage?

One of the biggest fashion faux paus women make is choosing fashion that is age inappropriate. Older women choose fashions too young and actually make them look older. A younger woman just entering the business world and wanting to look conservative will often select fashion that is much too old and she ends up looking frumpy.

Another fashion faux paus women make is choosing clothing that may be the latest trend, yet is way too sexy for work. Just because fashion magazines show a woman in a suit with a camisole or bustier worn underneath instead of a shirt, doesn't mean it is appropriate for the business world. If you were to take off your jacket, as the fashion magazines suggest, and attend a business dinner or social business event, you would be sending all the wrong signals. Never make someone wonder, "What is she selling?" The same is true for "bling jeans." If you have rhinestones on your pockets, what are people looking at? Do you want your business colleagues looking at your behind? My vote is No! You want them noticing you for your brain and your contribution. If they are looking at your behind, they are paying too much attention to the wrong asset.

## WHAT DOES YOUR COMMUNICATION SAY ABOUT YOU?

Administrative assistants spend a great deal of time interacting with a lot of clients internally and externally. Your ability to interact in a professional manner weighs heavily on your promotability and success. If your management is assured you represent the company and the team in a positive light, is confident your interpersonal skills are equivalent to management, and you can speak about your company and your region intelligently, you will be remembered as a professional. If you cannot demonstrate these behaviors, it can hold you back from moving forward in your career.

Some people refer to this as business protocol or business etiquette. It is simply making others feel comfortable enough with you that they trust you and want to do business with you.

While attending a meeting, I observed individuals as they walked into the room. It was interesting watching how some entered confidently and with assurance, conveying calmness in their movements. The individuals who really stood out were the ones who walked into the room as if they were saying, "I'd rather be having a root canal than be in this meeting!" Their posture conveyed a lack of confidence and credibility. The way they walked communicated hesitation and uncertainty. Their entire presence had an, "I don't care" type of attitude.

We may be very surprised, if we could see what others see about us when we enter a room, or participate in a meeting or a face-to-face conversation. It's very difficult to see yourself! We may feel we are communicating in a certain manner, and yet, the message we are giving others isn't what we intended. We may feel we are smiling and if we could see a picture of ourselves, we learn we had a scowl on our face as we were focusing on the message. These subtle gestures and comments can make a big impact.

If you want to be taken more seriously and have more impact and influence, concentrate on your body language.

Have you ever been in a room and literally "felt" someone's presence enter the room long before you heard him or her speak? We can feel our spirit being lifted in a positive way when someone enters the room, or feel a sense of relief when he or she leaves. Do you walk into a room like you belong there? Does your posture communicate confidence or uncertainty? Do you focus on uplifting others and being helpful?

We've all observed "put together, sharp looking" individuals enter a room with confidence. They tell others through their body language they know where they're going. Well, chances are these people weren't always this way. Chances are they learned this behavior and you can, too.

We need to develop our self-awareness and understand how we are perceived by others. I highly recommend enlisting the help of supportive friends by asking them for candid feedback. Ask them how you are perceived. Listen for the positive comments about what you are doing well and how it affects others. Listen for feedback suggesting room for improvement. The feedback may surprise you or be hard to hear; however, when your friends are sharing feedback, they are sharing the information because they care about you and want you to succeed.

## BODY LANGUAGE

Let's focus on making a positive impression on others by using positive body language techniques. The first step is to understand we communicate with our energy, attitude, body language and spoken words. More than half of all one-on-one communication is nonverbal.

I once worked with someone who did a great job of wordsmithing his messages, but his words and body language didn't match. Therefore, his message wasn't understood. People didn't trust him and didn't think he was authentic. When our verbal and nonverbal communication isn't aligned, we create confusion and resistance.

**Listen:** One of the best ways to have positive communication with others is to listen. You may think you need to be an expert conversationalist and have all sorts of clever topics to share. When you take the time to listen and let others talk about themselves, you'll find they'll actually remember you more than if you were the one doing all the talking!

Demonstrate you are listening by leaning in and turning your head, torso and body towards the person who is speaking. Nod or tilt your head to demonstrate you are engaged in the conversation while listening to the message. When your body is turned away from the person with whom you are talking, it can appear disrespectful, as though you don't buy into what they are saying, or are disinterested in the subject. Remember, it's important to hear people and it is just as important to make sure they know you are listening.

**Make eye contact:** It shows respect, confidence and engagement. When we avoid eye contact, it can signal deception. When you look down instead of looking someone in the eye, it appears you are uncomfortable, self-conscious or have something to hide. Also, be careful not to make eye contact for so long it becomes a "stare down" competition.

**Smile:** A simple smile conveys you are approachable, trustworthy, and cooperative. It also directly influences how others respond to you. The next time you are in the checkout line in the grocery store, take a moment to smile in an authentic way. You'll be surprised how much more customer service you receive when you have a genuine smile on your face. When we smile at others, they almost always smile in return. When we smile, it triggers a corresponding feeling and sense of happiness. We've actually caused a positive effect on their emotional state. Your body should communicate credibility, so the last thing you want to do is fake it. If your smile isn't genuine, it will communicate you are disingenuous.

**Tone of Voice:** Use a lower tone of voice, by breathing through your diaphragm instead of using a higher pitched voice caused by breathing high in the chest. I've noticed a lot of women raising their pitch at the end of their sentences, which turns their comment into a question. Be careful not to use this approach as it decreases the strength of your comment.

**Remove Barriers:** When you are having a conversation with someone and there is something physical between you and the other person that is blocking your view, such as a laptop or a large centerpiece, move the item or position yourself so there is no longer a physical barrier between you and the other person. It may seem trivial; however, it can be a barrier limiting your collaboration.

**Respect Boundaries:** We all have our own imaginary space bubble or comfort zone. When others enter our personal space, we become uncomfortable. A general rule of thumb is to keep a distance of an arm's length away. By honoring this space, you are demonstrating respect for others personal boundaries.

**Keep Open:** It has long been recognized that if your arms are crossed in front of you, others may view you as being closed off to them or their ideas. Did you know that we remember less if our arms and legs are closed than if we have unfolded arms and legs? Isn't it interesting? We've heard for years to not fold our arms because it makes us look closed off and guess what? Our body already knew having our arms and legs folded closes us off to receiving messages. Having open body language conveys approachability

**Posture**: Stand up straight, with your head up and shoulders back. Your feet should be shoulder width apart. Standing and sitting with good posture conveys self-respect, confidence, strength and stamina.

**Mirror Behavior:** Mirroring the person you are talking with is a great way to increase your relate-ability factor. It's a way to communicate you are like them or agree with what they are saying. To mirror, pay attention to the body language and gestures of the other person. Then, subtly demonstrate the same. If they are smiling, smile. If they are expressive in their facial gestures, reciprocate the expressiveness. If they are reserved, demonstrate a calm reserved presence. Mirroring others is a method to show you "speak their language" and will help you build rapport quickly.

**Distracting Behaviors:** Avoid distracting behaviors as your listener will focus on what you are doing rather than listening to what you are saying. A co-worker of mine had a habit of waiving her arms around up high and motioning from side to side, as if she were directing an airplane on the tarmac. I would catch myself looking in the direction she was pointing, trying to understand her message instead of listening to her words. The result: I was distracted and completely lost track of what she was saying.

Avoid distracting behaviors such as:

1. Crossing or folding your arms – appears you are closed off.

2. Fidgeting: putting your hands in your pockets and playing with whatever is inside of your pocket, playing with your hair or jewelry, adjusting your clothing – appears you are uncomfortable, distracted or have anxiety.

3. Using wild arm and hand gestures – appears nervous, lost and confused.

4. Overly smiling or nodding – appears novice, or junior and you don't understand how to communicate professionally. You don't want to look like a bobble head.

5. Frowning – appears you are unhappy or disagree.

6. Checking text messages emails, and social media – shows arrogance, disinterest and disrespect.

Effective body language is an essential aspect of effective communication. Whether unconscious or not, our body language affects our minds, our communication, and our relationships. Body language is powerful!

## WHAT DOES YOUR ATTITUDE SAY ABOUT YOU?

When I was in my early 20's, I began reading self-help books and fell in love with authors like Norman Vincent Peale, Dale Carnegie and John Maxwell. My husband and I read frequently and the messages nourished us like water being poured onto seedlings. We drank it up! We made notes in the margins and highlighted the messages that spoke to us. Some of our books are almost entirely filled with highlighter!

The positive messages made a difference in our lives. We read, "When the student is ready, the teacher appears." My husband and I had become students of the positive mental attitude way of life. We firmly believe we wouldn't be in leadership positions today if we weren't "students" early on in our careers. To this day, we seek out these types of authors and messages.

Neither my husband nor I have college degrees and yet, we are both in positions of leadership. We are both involved in our community and are asked to lead others. We challenge ourselves to continue growing and stretch ourselves by saying "yes" to opportunities which come our way. Even when we don't have the experience or background to answer the call to leadership; we accept it and find a way to be successful. You can too!

If you are going to be successful in this world, you must have enough positive energy to overcome the many negative attitudes and circumstances you will face. If you haven't developed this skill, you will face defeat quickly. It's not your manager's job to pick you up when you are down. It's not your co-workers job to encourage you day after day because you aren't being treated the way you'd like. It's your job to manage you and your emotions. You need to find a source of strength and optimism that will sustain you during these difficult times.

My advice is to read and listen to information and positive messages to build yourself up mentally and emotionally. As administrative assistants, we are often in the positions of counselors and advisors. Staff members come to us and want to vent about a particular situation. We need to be strong enough to listen with empathy and not let the message weigh us down negatively. There will be times when boundaries need to be established to prevent us from being used as a crutch for someone else's negative behavior and get caught in the downward energy spiral while listening to their problems.

# Networking:
# It's All About Connecting

"The time to build a network
isn't when you need one!"

CHAPTER**THREE**

# Networking: It's All About Connecting

D o you cringe when you hear the word, "Networking?" Are you excited when your manager or colleague invites you to a networking event? I was probably in my early twenties when I heard the word "networking" for the first time.

I've always been very social and enjoyed meeting new people. Even so, I was pretty nervous attending my first business meeting for the purposes of networking outside of the office. I wasn't sure what to do, or if what I was doing was right or appropriate. More than likely, I was fidgeting with my hair or jewelry and displaying a whole host of awkward body language. I'm pretty sure I was an insecure and hesitant mess! Well, guess what. Twenty years later, I found out this is how most people feel!

Here's our likely networking invitation scenario: We're at work doing our typical routine; screening calls, preparing our managers and ourselves for meetings, attending meetings, triaging email, creating presentations, summarizing reports, gathering information, greeting guests and making travel arrangements (*to name a few of our daily tasks*) when out of nowhere, it hits us! We come across the dreaded email regarding an upcoming networking event. We quickly open our calendar and hope we're booked. Our heart skips a beat as we see our schedule is wide open! Our blood pressure begins to rise and nervous tension builds...and then our clever minds immediately employ our best and brightest creative and strategic skills with enough fierceness to stop a small army to create our response.

### We respond with our decline:

"Thank you for your invitation to the
*(insert your dreaded networking event name here);*
due to previous commitments I am unable to attend.
I wish you much success at your upcoming event."

Like magic, we're off the hook! But, are we really? Did we luck out or miss out?

When we "miss out," we miss out on the opportunity to connect with others and to establish a relationship. The whole purpose of networking is to create a connection. It's an opportunity to genuinely discover information about others, get to know them and determine if you can establish authentic connections. Once a connection has begun, it's important to nourish the relationship. When this happens, you'll experience some give and take naturally happening. When the relationship has been developed and an opportunity arises where one of you needs something, it is completely appropriate to ask for his or her help. This is what I refer to as the serendipitous moment. This only occurs when you have created a connection and nourished the relationship. If you ask for help too early, it appears the only reason you are networking is to get your needs met. The key is: relationships are king. The relationship should always be considered before business.

## NETWORKING FEARS:

Typically, fear is what holds us back from wanting to network. Some of the top fears of networking are:

1. Fear of rejection

2. Fear of our ability to start a conversation

3. Fear of not knowing anyone

4. Fear of not dressing appropriately

5. Fear of getting out of our comfort zone

Often, our fear is due to low confidence levels based on one or more of the above.

## NETWORKING UNSPOKEN RULES

Looking back at my first networking experience, I wish I would've known then what I know now. Here are some of the "unspoken" rules of networking I've learned over the years:

1. Don't crash a connection. If you see two people intently engaged and talking, don't interrupt them by joining their circle. Instead, look for those who are alone or in groups of three or more.

2. Don't monopolize anyone's time. Talk to someone for five to ten minutes, then move on to talk to someone else.

3. Don't ask for a job or a favor.

4. Do offer to help someone who needs your expertise.

5. Don't over indulge in alcohol, stick to a one drink maximum.

6. Do wear business attire.

7. Bring your business cards and paper or electronic calendar.

8. Bring a positive attitude.

9. Wear a smile.

10. If you aren't connecting, don't stay stuck!

## WHAT DO YOU DO IF YOU GET STUCK?

If you find yourself in a completely awkward situation, you can easily employ the *"Graceful Exit" or the "Respectful Reminder."*

### Graceful Exit:
"Thank you for sharing. It was nice talking with you. Talk to you soon."
Then, make an exit to the buffet or to another person.

### Respectful Reminder:
"It was great catching up with you; I always enjoy talking with you.
I promised myself to make sure and meet someone new tonight.
Let's talk again soon."

Then, make an exit to meet a new connection. You don't have to stay in an awkward situation. That's the beauty of networking; it's like speed dating without dating the person. You get to introduce yourself to someone new, explore the possibility of a connection, and if you aren't connecting, find someone else to talk with and create a connection.

## AWKWARD AND CHALLENGING SITUATIONS

Another reason people dread going to networking events is due to the awkward networkers, referred to as "Connector Deflectors." These are the types of behaviors we all want to avoid because they make us feel uncomfortable. These behaviors definitely fall in the "what not to do" category.

## "INGRID – THE INTERRUPTER"

What do you do with someone who is constantly interrupting you? You have a handful of choices depending upon the situation.

If it's a one-on-one conversation:

1. Listen.

2. Continue talking and let the one who talks the longest and loudest win.

3. Accept the behavior, knowing she is overly excited and engaged in the conversation.

4. Provide honest feedback regarding behavior.

If it's a group of three or more:

1. Listen.

2. Continue talking and let the one who talks the longest and loudest win.

3. Accept her behavior, knowing she is overly excited and engaged in the conversation.

4. Ignore her.

5. Introduce her to the rest of the group and then continue with your comments, include her in the conversation.

## "ONE WAY – CHARLIE"

I'm sure you've experienced the person who dominates the conversation. He may ask you a question, yet, he doesn't give you the opportunity to answer. Instead he just keeps on talking. You simply can't get a word in! He's the one way conversationalist.

What do you do with someone who dominates the conversation?

1. If he is someone you really want to know or need to know, listen.

2. If not, employ the "Graceful Exit" or the "Respectful Reminder."

## "KEVIN – THE KIDNAPPER AND HIS FRIEND, MARVIN – THE MONOPOLIZER"

These are the types of people who corner you at a networking event, monopolize your time and make it difficult to get away. Remember, networking events aren't meant for anyone to dominate anyone's time. Be aware how long you've been talking with someone, even if it's going well.

What do you do if it's going well?

1. Engage the "Graceful Exit" or "Respectful Reminder" and if they prompt you to linger, do so, if you choose.

2. If you engage the "Graceful Exit" or "Respectful Reminder" and they don't ask you to linger, don't take it negatively. Move on to another connection. You don't want to hold anyone hostage, no matter how well the conversation is going. Instead, ask to

follow up with them later to meet for coffee to
continue the conversation. Then, make sure
you follow up!

## "GARY – GET OVER YOURSELF ALREADY"

This person is enamored with himself. It's all about his car, home,
vacation, job, success, etc. He is the type of person who is a
name dropper, compares himself to others and always wants to
be better than everyone else.

What do you do with someone who is constantly trying to im-
press you?

1. Listen and nod.

2. Genuinely buy into the entertainment and
   enjoy it.

3. Learn from the experience of what not to do
   and what doesn't work.

4. If you are repulsed by his behavior, employ the
   "Graceful Exit" or "Respectful Reminder" and
   move on to your next connection.

## "CLIQUES AND MEAN GIRLS"

We all know these girls, don't we? First and foremost, this is not
about you. This is about their insecurities and comfort zones.

How do you handle cliques?

1. Be gracious.

2. Be confident.

3.  Be professional.

4.  Be authentic.

Realize you will meet people at networking events, or anywhere in your life, for that matter, with whom you aren't going to want to connect based on their values, character and authenticity. That's okay. The reason we have networking events is to meet people, and see if they are people with whom we want to connect. When we realize we don't want to connect, we don't need to spend the evening with them. Remember, you are there for authentic connections. If you can't make a connection, move on.

You may find the "mean girl" behavior was just an act to deal with insecurities. If you had a chance to get to know one of them, you'd likely find a completely delightful person. If you think there's a chance of this being true, approach her one-on-one. It's much harder to break into a tight circle. You'll have to watch for just the right moment to approach them in an authentic natural way. Perhaps one of them arrives before the rest of the group and you can greet her with a warm hello. Or perhaps one of them happens to be in the buffet line alone and you can strike up a conversation there. One of the best ways to connect and really get to know someone is by volunteering. If she is involved with a non-profit community activity, offer to help her. She'll appreciate you getting involved and you'll see her in a completely different light.

## "RUFUS – THE REJECTER"

This is the biggest fear of networking. We all want to be accepted and liked by others. No one wants to be rejected. What can you do so you won't be rejected? Well…there is no magic answer! We all get rejected. It happens to everyone. Remember, the point of networking is to make a connection. If a connection isn't happening, don't take it personal. Who knows what might be going on in someone else's life? It more than likely isn't about you.

**A word of advice:**
If one person rejects you: be polite, positive, and professional, and move on to your next connection.

If five or more people reject you: do a quick assessment. You may be practicing some of the "Connector Deflector" behaviors and need to tweak your approach.

## CONVERSATION STARTERS

Here's the secret to being comfortable at networking events, you need to know how to start a conversation. This is the art of engaging conversation. Some people have the gift of gab and can easily talk to strangers. Even so, talking doesn't mean you are connecting.

I was at a football game, in a private skybox (due to networking) and observed two men who were meeting for the first time. They shook hands and introduced themselves in a natural and appropriate interaction. It was relaxed and a perfect moment to begin getting to know each other. However, that is not what happened. What took place was an awkward and disingenuous approach. One person started asking questions using the rapid fire method …one question asked on top of the other without a moment for the other person to answer. The questions seemed to be aimed at finding out if the other person could be useful to his career and his own interests. It quickly became unnatural and awkward. The person being asked the questions took a step backward to provide more distance and air cover to create a barrier between Mr. Rapid Fire and himself. When someone takes a step back, his feet are doing the talking. His body language is saying he doesn't feel safe and doesn't want to engage.

To network effectively, you want to ask open-ended questions that naturally lead to more dialogue, questions, and connection. It's very important for these questions to be authentic and not merely a rapid fire battering. You'll want to ask a question, pause, listen to the answer, and learn about the other person. Use responses, clarifying questions and the information being shared to build on the conversation. Use open-ended questions that begin with "starters" instead of "stoppers:"

**Starters: Who, What, When, Where, Why and How**

**Stoppers: Is, Would, Could, Should, Do**

Here are some examples of open-ended questions:

1. How long have you lived in the area?

2. When you're not working, what is your favorite thing to do?

3. What most intrigued you about coming today?

4. What are you most proud about in your career?

5. What do you like most about what you do?

Use questions that feel genuine to you. Create authentic, open-ended questions that work for you and your personality.

It's more important to be interested than to be interesting.

## FOCUS ON OTHERS

Everyone wants to be listened to and heard. When people know someone is listening, they generally open up and share a lot about themselves. When you ask a question, pay attention, get engaged in active listening, and do all you can to learn about the other person's interests. Lean in and say, "That's interesting. Tell me more." When you use this approach in an authentic way, the other person starts to relax and open up and you get information about his or her desires, passions, ideas and challenges. Consider how you may be able to help with something he or she shared with you, such as a contact you may have, or an idea based on your experience. Be a resource.

My husband is a master at this approach. People will often compliment him on being a great conversationalist. We always laugh later as he mainly asks questions and listens.

# Remember, if you can get the other person to talk, you will be the one remembered.

## DO YOUR RESEARCH

Do your research before attending a networking event. Find out who is attending by looking at the email distribution list, Facebook invite or, ask the host. Then, take a moment to review the list of attendees:

1. Do you know anyone attending?

2. Are you familiar with any of the guests or their names?

3. Are you familiar with any of their businesses or business names?

Next, discover what you can learn online by searching for an individual or business name. Look at social media accounts. You'll be amazed at what information you can gather.

When you show up "in the know" at a networking event, starting conversations is so much easier. You'll know what people are interested in and you'll know what topics you can discuss to quickly build rapport.

## HANDSHAKE

Did you know we've been shaking hands since the fifth century? One theory is the act of shaking hands signaled you had come in peace and didn't have a weapon. Did you know if you shake hands with people, they are more likely to remember you and they will be more open and friendly? Don't discount the simple gesture of shaking hands. When done right, it creates a lasting and positive impression.

You want a firm, web-to-web handshake; make eye contact, and a short up and down pump. Shaking hands in this manner communicates confidence. A limp handshake communicates weakness and a lack of confidence. When someone squeezes a hand too tightly, it is considered a control move. If you shake someone's hand and offer more than three pumps, it's considered amateur.

## INTRODUCTION MAKEOVER

In our roles as administrative assistants, we often act as greeters for our manager's guests. Make a positive impression by representing yourself well. When introducing yourself to someone, make it interesting. Instead of saying, "Hello, my name is (Your Name); I'm the Chief Executive Assistant to the (Title of person you support and company name)," try something more creative and memorable, such as "Hello. Welcome to (name of company). I do my best to manage the company by providing support to our top executive; my name is (Your Name.)"

Keep your introduction genuine and authentic, keep it real and be yourself. Being creative and saying your name last helps people remember you and your name. Remember, titles can be illusive and said so commonly that no one is listening. Instead of using your title, provide insight into what you do. Your approach will be intriguing and cause the other person to listen.

"There ain't no point in talking when no one is listening any way."

**–ROD STEWART**

Other than your appearance and handshake, your first impression is based on how well you introduce yourself. Your introduction needs to roll off your tongue with ease, confidence and authenticity. Many refer to this introduction as an "elevator speech" or your 30 second commercial. The reason it is called an elevator speech is because you should be able to give your 30 second commercial in an elevator in the time it takes you to reach the next floor.

Your 30 second commercial should include a "what" and a "why" about you. The "what" is a statement about you that takes no longer than 30 seconds to verbalize. It can be about:

1. What you do for a living.

2. How you add value to your customers.

3. How you help others succeed.

4. What you are passionate about.

5. What you strive to be.

The "why" is what you want to quickly disclose and/or describe about who you are and what you are about. Your 30 second commercial should end with a question to promote dialogue and create a connection. Example: *"Hello, I'm in the research and development industry. What I'm really passionate about is helping people be successful. My name is (Insert name her). How can I help you?"*

## OVERCOME YOUR FEARS AND DISCOMFORT

Never miss a chance to network. You may feel awkward when you first begin networking. Realize practicing and pushing through the awkward stage is part of a growing process and the more you put yourself in a networking environment, the more comfortable you will become.

Networking is simply interacting with people to develop a connection and build a relationship. Don't be so afraid of failure that you don't show up. Never let the fear of striking out keep you from playing the game.

**To increase your confidence, prepare with a goal in mind:**

1. Face Your Fear: Commit to the event, do your research, know something about attendees.

2.  Suit Up: Determine your wardrobe. Put on a positive attitude and a smile and bring your business cards.

3.  Confidence: Know why you are attending. Focus on your goal and others. Practice your 30 second introduction.

4.  Show Up: Have fresh breath and clean teeth.

5.  Get Your Game On: Use engaging conversation, have a natural introduction and 30 second commercial. Mingle, standing tall, use positive body language. Be polite, look put together, practice self-awareness, and look for connections.

6.  Make a Genuine Connection: Build rapport with someone, discover commonality, and truly listen.

7.  Make the Pass: When a connection occurs, pass your business card and ask for the other person's business card.

8.  Follow Up: Send a handwritten note and enclose your business card.

9.  Call: Schedule coffee, lunch or another meeting to continue the connection.

## BE INCLUSIVE

In the beginning, there will be times when you find yourself alone at networking events. As you increase your connections, you'll rarely experience being alone again. Pay attention to those around you. If you see someone alone, invite him or her to join your group. Take the time to introduce him or her to others inside and outside of your group. Help make connections for him or her with others you know.

I had the good fortune of having someone do this for me. She is one of the nicest people you'd ever meet. She's also very connected within our community. Whenever I saw her at networking events, she always walked up to me, shook my hand and genuinely welcomed me to the event. She acted as if the event was her private party and she wanted to make sure everyone there was having a good time and was making plenty of connections within the room. We would chat for a few minutes and then she would say, "There's someone I want you to meet." She would walk me over to a group of people and politely introduce me to the group by telling them a little bit about me. She always tailored her message by including aspects about me that were of interest to that new group or person. She did the same for me by introducing them to me and tailoring her message to bring out aspects of the group or person that were of interest to me. She was a master connector. I can't recall another person who has ever done this for me or for others in my presence. I will always be thankful for her approach and her interest in others. Due to her gracious approach, I met a lot of wonderful people with whom I am still connected. I also consider her one of my dearest friends.

## People never forget someone who made them feel welcome.

### THE FOLLOW UP:

**Remember People:** After the event has concluded and you are back at your office or home, take the time to scan through the business cards you collected. If you don't have a business card for everyone you met, use a plain piece of paper. Write down everything you can remember about the person: What he/she looked like; how he or she was dressed; if he/she had children; where he/she was going on vacation; if he/she is involved in a new venture; how he/she contributes to your community; etc. This action will help you remember people's names. It's also a great idea to record this information in your "outlook contacts" for quick reference. The next time a networking event comes up, you'll have a quick resource to refresh yourself on all the people you previously met and on the past conversations. When you bring up information shared during a past conversation, or something of interest to them, it will tell them you were listening and they matter to you. It will make a very positive impression.

**Handwritten Note:** A day or two after the event, make a positive and memorable impression by sending a handwritten note in a nice card to the people you met. Not an email, but a handwritten note. Include a message regarding your previous discussion and drop in your business card (even if you already exchanged business cards at the event.) The person may have misplaced your card. You want to make it as easy as possible to connect with you. To really make a positive impression, recall an interest that your new contact discussed, tear out an article you just read from a trade magazine, or print an article regarding a topic of interest, and enclose it with your note. People rarely send handwritten notes any more or offer information to help someone who is a new acquaintance. Never discount how much this small gesture can have on a future connection.

### Quick Reminder: Do's:

1. Walk into the event with confidence. I have found more often than not, administrative

assistants aren't as confident as they should be. Let me share a quote with you about confidence by psychologist, Rosabeth Moss Kanter: *"Confidence consists of positive expectations for favorable outcomes. Confidence influences the willingness to invest. Every step we take, every investment we make, is based on whether we feel we can count on ourselves and others to accomplish what has been promised. Confidence determines whether our steps are tiny and tentative or big and bold."* In summary, Rosabeth is saying confidence is based on our ability to accomplish what we've promised. The administrative assistants I know, deliver! Be confident in yourself and your abilities.

2. Walk in with a calm attitude. When you are calm, it will help others be calm around you.

3. Stand up straight with your shoulders back and your feet shoulder width apart.

4. Speak with a lower tone of voice, breathe from your diaphragm.

5. Make eye contact and smile!

## Quick Reminder: Don't Use Distracting Behaviors

1. Crossing or folding your arms.

2. Putting your hands in your pockets and fidgeting with the contents.

3.  Standing in a protective state by covering yourself in a "fig leaf" position.

4.  Playing with your hair or your jewelry.

5.  Overly smiling or nodding your head.

I attended my first Administrative Professional's Conference in 2003. I was absolutely captivated with the entire experience from the vast size of the ballroom and thousands of attendees to the packed agenda with an overwhelming amount of breakout sessions. I sat in amazement as I listened. I took copious notes trying to take it all in. I wanted to get as much as I could out of the event.

I began networking with attendees outside of my company, with those who worked for the event company and with a few speakers. To my surprise, everyone (including the speakers) was incredibly receptive. I'm not sure what I was expecting. I was just relieved everyone was so open to having a conversation and learning more about each other.

I had the good fortune of attending a conference the following year as well, and this time, I was more prepared. I created index cards with questions for fellow attendees. This allowed me to quickly engage and gather benchmarking information. I had more confidence and grace when I approached the event company staff. I thanked them for the event. It was fun seeing some of the same faces I had seen from the previous year. I was more comfortable approaching the speakers as I thanked them for the information they shared and struck up conversations about the workshops. I was bold and asked if they had time for a cup of coffee, glass of wine, or their favorite beverage. I've continued to do this at each and every conference I've attended. My network grew and I learned a great deal from administrative colleagues from across the country, conference management staff, and the speakers.

For each new connection, I created "Outlook Contacts" so I could record the names, company and contact information, and anything I could remember about them such as their interests, if they had children, and what type of administrative work they performed.

To foster the connection, I stayed in touch by emailing my contacts a quick hello, sharing relevant information I had read and finding out if they would be at the next conference so we could re-connect. As time went on, these contacts shared relevant information with me and we shared best practices with each other as well.

I am honored to say many of these connections are still thriving and growing strong. In fact, due to many of these connections, I have continued to grow in ways I couldn't have managed by myself, such as becoming an author and a speaker.

Today, there are many social networks available which enable new and established connections to grow. We can easily become LinkedIn associates or Facebook Friends and learn about people's interests, involvement, goals, thoughts, and pursuits and have tremendous insight even though we've just met! Take advantage of these tools. You'll be amazed how helpful they can be to building connections.

In summary, network successfully by focusing on making a fabulous first impression, creating a connection, and developing rapport. This will build lasting relationships.

There are relationships built on the real you, and there's everything else.

# The Power of Gratitude

"The root of joy is gratefulness!"

**–DAVID STEINDL-RAST**

CHAPTER**FOUR**

# The Power of Gratitude

Have you ever noticed when you complain about something that isn't going well, there's always someone who will jump on board with you? As a result, you feel connected. Is this the type of connection you really want? Do you want to create a connection built upon negativity? If we're not careful, this behavior can become a habit. As we complain or listen to others complain, our energy levels drop and our outlook becomes bleak.

Complaining is the dividing wall between the life you have and the life you want to have.

Gratitude breaks down this wall.

Let me ask you another question. Have you ever noticed how good you feel when you are around someone who is genuinely grateful? I have, and I absolutely love it! My whole mood is lifted up. I feel lighter, freer and have more energy. I'm more creative. My outlook tends to match his/her grateful attitude and as a result, the connection I make with the other person is based upon positive thoughts, creative energy, and an urge to pull each other to a higher place than we were before we interacted.

Having an attitude of gratitude actually kills self-pity, jealousy, bitterness, regret, and negative thoughts. More often than not, the thing that holds us back more than anything else is our own negative thinking and negative self-talk. We all have negative thoughts from time to time. However, focusing on gratitude will help diffuse the negativity and propel us forward.

One of the best ways to become filled with an attitude of gratitude is to start keeping a gratitude journal. There are a number of ways you can keep a gratitude journal. You can record something you are grateful for each day on Facebook and ask your friends and family to join you in a 30 day gratitude challenge. You can get creative, make a journal, and fill it with writing about moments you are grateful for and include pictures of things that make you feel grateful.

You may doubt how transformational this simple act can be on your life. You may be skeptical. Professor Emmons of the University of California did a study of a group of people who kept gratitude journals. He found that in just three weeks there was a direct positive effect on those who kept the journals. What is even more impressive is the positive effects lasted for several months after the three week period ended. The people in the study exercised more, drank less alcohol, and their friends and family noticed they were nicer to be around. Imagine what a difference a gratitude journal could make in your life if you chose to participate for 6 weeks!

Developing an attitude of gratitude will transform your life and will provide you with tremendous strength to withstand future challenges. I have found no matter how bad things may seem, the simple act of writing about things for which I'm thankful shifts my mood and focus. It takes a conscious effort to be positive and focus on why you should feel grateful.

# Grat·i·tude [**grat**-i-tood] *noun*,
# The state of being grateful;
# a feeling of thankfulness or appreciation.

Take a moment right now to write down 10 things for which you are grateful. They can be big or small.

1. _____

2. _____

3. _____

4. _____

5. _____

6 _____

7. _____

8. _____

9. _____

10. _____

When I talk about being positive and having an attitude of gratitude, some people think I have a perfect life, perfect home, and a perfect family. Well, that couldn't be further from the truth. I've faced many challenges in my life. I know what it feels like to lose family members to cancer, drugs, and alcohol. I know what it feels like to be worried about financial peril. I know how it feels to have a son in the military deployed to a war zone and not be able to talk to him for several days. I know how it feels to lie awake at 3:00 am with tears streaming down my cheeks from the pain of a heartbreak so intense I couldn't sleep all night and had to go to work in the morning.

I'm currently facing one of the most difficult challenges I have experienced in my life.

I was at work on a busy Monday morning beginning with the Executive Committee Meeting and subsequent actions following the meeting. I took a quick break to look at my phone and noticed I had missed a call from my daughter-in-law, Wilikinia (Wili), who was contacting me about my 1½ year old grandson, Damon. When she couldn't reach me, she sent me a text that read:

"In ER with Damon.
They are running tests.
Will send more info when we get it. Prayers, please!"

My first thought was Damon probably had another ear infection and would be fine. Not to worry. He had been having a round of ear infections, sore throats, minor bruises here and there, and recently, had tiny red dots on his legs. Overall, he had been sick off and on for a while, but nothing serious. We chalked it up to being in day care and part of a normal childhood. I went to the restroom and as I walked back to my office, I had a strong feeling I needed to go to the emergency room. I wasn't sure why, as this isn't something I would normally do unless it was serious. I was in the middle of explaining the situation to my co-worker, Denise, when I got a call from my husband, René, who was calling from the Emergency Room, which also wasn't typical. I could hear the worry in his voice as he told me the ER doctor thought our grandson, Damon, may have meningitis and the doctor was considering airlifting him to Spokane to the Sacred Heart Children's Hospital.

My heart sank! I sprang up from my desk and told my manager, Mike, that I needed to leave and before I could explain, tears started to flow. Mike quickly and supportively said, "Go! Get out of here." I immediately left the office and started to drive to the hospital. I called my husband to let him know I was on my way but wasn't able to reach him. I continued to call, still no answer. I feared they had already taken Damon to Spokane. I called Wili and my son, Matthew. Again, no answer. I, then, received a call from Rene' and he said the words no one wants to ever hear,

> "Honey, they think Damon may have leukemia and
> they are airlifting him to Spokane."

I told René I was on my way and I would hurry. As I hung up the phone, the tears started flowing. I prayed a desperate prayer and begged God not to take Damon from us. I asked God to cure Damon of all diseases and wrap His love and strength around him and our family to comfort us and keep us strong.

The tears were flowing uncontrollably. I knew I needed to talk to someone to help calm my nerves before arriving at the hospital so I could be strong for my family, especially Matthew and Wili.

I called Denise and she told me not to panic, Damon hadn't been diagnosed yet, to be calm while I drove, and she would pray for me. I, then, called my friend, Debbie. She also provided encouragement, love, and support. I drove as fast as I could to Our Lady of Lourdes Emergency Room. I was so worried I would miss seeing Damon before they had to leave. When I arrived, Wili was holding Damon who already had an IV in his arm. He was crying and scared. Matthew, Wili, and René all looked scared, a little numb and in shock. We were all doing our best to be strong, positive, and support each other.

The gurney was in the hallway and the Medstar flight crew was preparing Damon for the flight. They strapped Damon onto the gurney and wheeled him and Wili to the helicopter. Matthew, René, and I walked out to the helipad area and watched as they boarded the helicopter and flew off to Spokane.

It all happened so fast. My mind was racing with questions and my heart was full of emotions which I was keeping bottled up inside of me to help keep everyone else strong, when all I wanted to do was fall apart and bawl like a baby.

René, Matthew, and I had driven to the hospital in our own cars, so we left separately to go home and pack a few things, and make a few quick arrangements before we left for Spokane together.

When we arrived at Sacred Heart Children's Hospital, we met Dr. Intzes. He seemed fairly certain Damon's diagnosis would be confirmed as leukemia. He needed to do further testing to confirm and would tell us the results soon. The hours dragged by and still no confirmation. Whenever Damon rested, we did our best to distract ourselves by visiting, playing games, and watching movies.

It was early evening when Dr. Intzes came by to advise us of the confirmed diagnosis. As he said the word "leukemia," I wanted to run out of the room to somehow escape the truth of it all. Another part of me wanted to yell and tell him he was wrong. I thought this couldn't be the truth! I looked at my children and saw their bodies shaking as the tears fell steadily down their cheeks. They held Damon and looked into his sweet face. I knew there was nothing any of us could do to change the diagnosis. Our only choice was to be strong. I did my best to keep my emotions in check so my children could lean on René and me and release their emotions.

It was by far one of the most raw and painful moments I have ever felt as a mother or grandmother. I knew in my heart this would be one of many yet to come. The doctor proceeded to tell us many things about treatment, side effects, and expectations. The best news was learning the type of leukemia Damon has, Acute Lymphoblastic Leukemia (ALL), has an 85% recovery rate, and they expect him to do well. The doctor predicted it to be a three and a half year journey which won't be easy, but it is possible.

As the doctor left, we all hugged one another and more tears flowed. It was extremely difficult to accept the diagnosis as our reality and listen to all the other information about the treatment plan and research program participation. It was overwhelming. As the mother of these children and grandmother of Damon, I wanted to tell them it would be okay. I wanted to do something to make it okay. All I could do was stay strong, offer words of encouragement, and show them love by continuing to stay with them at the hospital, providing hugs, preparing food, and doing laundry.

It's been six months since we learned Damon has leukemia. Initially, he was very sick. Due to the chemotherapy and side effects, he lost a lot of weight and strength. At times, he was so weak he couldn't squat down to pick up a toy and stand back up. There were even days when he could barely walk. Seeing his little legs shake and tears fall down his cheeks because of the pain was heartbreaking. It's been a long road, with three years left to go before he's fully recovered.

We've learned how to turn a hospital room into a dining room for a Thanksgiving feast and how to use an IV Pole as a base for a Christmas tree. We've learned how to make a meal in a micro-wave and how to pass time in the hospital room doing puzzles, playing cards, and watching movies. More than anything else, we have learned to support each other through some incredibly difficult moments.

All things considered, Damon is doing well and has improved greatly since those difficult days. At the moment, we have a short break before entering into "Delayed Intensification" which can include an 8-12 week hospital stay and some difficult side effects. Once we get through this hurdle, the next phase will be much easier.

We were a close family prior to facing this challenge and we've become even closer. We've learned how incredibly loving family, friends, and a community can be when you are the ones in the midst of a storm. The support of those in our lives, our faith, and our love for each other is what has brought us this far, as well as the incredible gratitude we have for each and every day we have with Damon and one another.

Adversity has a way of sharpening your priorities and making you realize how thankful you are for the wonderful people in your life. The challenges help you push away the clutter and focus more intently on what is really important to you. You become more aware of the everyday miracles that exist in your life and cherish the moments you experience.

The last time I did a gratitude journal was in the midst of road trips to Children's hospital and to the Ronald McDonald house to visit my grandson, son and daughter-in-law for a few days or for the weekend. You may think it would be difficult to find something to be grateful for in the midst of seeing your grandson struggle through chemotherapy. However, focusing on finding something to be grateful about is what saved me from feeling hopeless.

There is always,
always something
for which to be
thankful.

I encourage you to be thankful for the people you meet and those who are in your life. Relationships take time and energy. Nurture your relationships and don't take them for granted. You never know what challenges you may have to face in your life. People will never know how much you appreciate them until you tell them. Don't wait until it's too late. Let them know how much you love and appreciate them. Give your love and hugs freely and often.

So, what does all this have to do with being an administrative assistant? That's a good question! There are several reasons why an attitude of gratitude can make all the difference in your role as an administrative assistant and set you apart from the masses. I am incredibly thankful for the experiences I have had in my career as an administrative professional. My journey hasn't always been easy and as strange as it may sound, I am grateful for the struggle. The struggle has helped shape me into who I am and has provided me strength to handle difficult challenges. I've learned being positive in negative situations is not naïve, it's leadership. I've also learned how much better I feel when I talk about my blessings more than I talk about my burdens.

You interact with multitudes of people on a daily basis. Consider for a moment what other people may be going through. They might be involved in a huge challenge and you are the bright spot in their lives reminding them to be grateful.

When I am in a board room full of executives I can only imagine what they are going through in their personal lives, let alone handling difficult business decisions. Often, the executives seem tense due to the pressures of their responsibilities. It is in these moments that an act of kindness, something as simple as a smile, can go a long way. Don't discount this act as something trite. Kindness is often missing from the workplace and will serve you and others well in the long run.

If you've been working for the same company and in the same role for more than five years, you may not feel as grateful as you did when you first started. You may feel you've been slighted or looked over for a promotion. You may think your company or your manager owes you more than what you've received. When you start focusing on being grateful for what you have, your entire energy shifts and your performance increases.

What are you focusing on? Finding fault or finding something to appreciate and expressing gratitude? I'm not asking you to put on rose colored glasses and blindly look at a situation or discount a need for improvement. What I'm saying is when you become negative and feel your company or your manager owes you something, the energy you project isn't the type of energy a manager wants to reward. Instead, focus on the experiences, growth, benefits, and rewards you are thankful for and express your gratitude to your manager for those things. Trust me—your manager will likely be more interested in rewarding you if you convey a positive and grateful attitude.

Think about it this way. Do you want to reward a child who is constantly whining and complaining about things not being fair and wanting more than what they have? Or, are you more likely to reward a child who expresses gratitude and appreciation for what they have?

# The more you are in a state of gratitude, the more you will attract things to be grateful for.

You might be the one person who can see the silver lining in the midst of a difficult re-organization. Coming from a grateful perspective instead of a fearful perspective can create imaginative and resourceful thinking. Your energy can create a ripple effect of ideas that wouldn't exist without you.

I am thankful for having the opportunity to brainstorm with my administrative colleagues. On multiple occasions, the outcome was discovering new ways to operate and impact the bottom line in a substantial manner.

It's fascinating to observe a team feeling powerless becoming empowered as ideas are embraced. It's also extremely rewarding to share your ideas with management and see your ideas realized.

> Gratitude helps you grow and expand; gratitude brings joy and laughter into your life and into the lives of all those around you.

Someone who has a grateful attitude is more likely to send a thank you card. People rarely send handwritten thank you cards anymore. When you take the time to do so, it always makes a positive impression. Sending a thank you card to a customer, a manager, or a co-worker helps build loyalty. Too often, we underestimate the power of little acts of kindness.

As administrative assistants, we are often the ones who receive mail for those we support. When was the last time you or your manager received a handwritten thank you card? When was the last time you sent your manager a handwritten thank you card?

I am grateful for receiving thank you cards from my manager, staff, customers, community members, and administrative colleagues. I keep the cards as reminders that someone is grateful for something I've done.

# Feeling gratitude and not expressing it is like wrapping a present and not giving it.

Focusing on what we are grateful for creates an environment of clear priorities. We know who and what is really important in our lives. Therefore, we should strive for a harmonious work and life balance, which creates a healthy environment both at home and at work.

I am grateful for the wake up calls I've had in my life to remind me that life is not all about work and a career. I'm thankful that I've supported managers who feel the same way and demonstrate their value for their families.

I am also grateful for having managers who have supported my growth and development, who have stood behind me, and supported my efforts. I am grateful for the "admin champions" I've had in my life who have encouraged me and championed administrative development for me and my colleagues.

"When you practice gratefulness,
there's a sense of respect towards others."
**–THE DALAI LAMA**

When we are grateful, we are more likely to have a desire to give back. How we choose to give back can vary greatly depending on our circumstances. We may choose to give back in a philanthropic way, become a mentor to someone, or give our time to a non-profit organization.

I am grateful for the opportunity to attend training and for the encouragement to provide a "teach back" upon returning from my first conference. I am thankful for working in a training department and being able to soak up all the training materials and attend the training classes, which led to becoming a certified trainer. These experiences developed my passion of training and speaking, which I absolutely love and feel called to do. These passions were realized due to my role as an administrative assistant. I am so grateful for the experiences I have had.

> "No gesture is too small
> when done with gratitude."
>
> **–OPRAH**

A grateful attitude leads toward empowering others. I absolutely love observing someone who is empowering another person. People who have an attitude of gratitude have an inner strength and know there is enough room in this world for all of us to succeed. When you listen to another person and engage in rich dialogue, you'll discover how you can enable and empower them to where they want to go, or lead them to someone else who can.

I am grateful for experience and confidence. I am thankful for having an adventurous spirit and not being afraid to take a risk. I am grateful for the courage to be the voice for administrative colleagues. I am thankful for having the opportunity to create programs to honor administrative assistants and further their growth and development.

I am grateful for the wisdom and understanding that most opportunities don't come to us, instead we find the way to create the opportunity.

"I think a hero is any person really intent on making this a better place for all people."

**—MAYA ANGELOU**

## CALL TO ACTION!

Begin your 30 day attitude of gratitude challenge today! You'll be amazed at how much better you will feel. Remember what Professor Emmons discovered while researching a gratitude challenge… in just three weeks there was a direct positive effect on those who kept a gratitude journal, and what's even more impressive is the positive effects lasted for several months after the three week period. If you are an overachiever, I challenge you to a 60 day attitude of gratitude challenge!

We must never forget
the importance of gratitude.
Say thank you when your heart is
full and when it breaks and when
you are alone and sad and when
you dance with joy and when
things are lost and found again.
Day and night give thanks for
this incredibly beautiful,
tragic gift called life.

# Choose Me!

"When you are asked if you can do a job,
tell 'em, 'Certainly I can!'
Then get busy and find out how to do it."

**—THEODORE ROOSEVELT**

CHAPTER**FIVE**

# Choose Me!

I had approximately 10 years of experience in the administrative field. I've held many positions over my career. I'd been a secretary for a small furniture company, a receptionist for an ophthalmologist which meant I was the scheduler, the bookkeeper, the janitor, and his assistant for minor surgeries in the office. I'd also been an office manager for an agriculture commission and association where I was their only support professional and managed the office, did financial reports and taxes, payroll, accounts receivable, accounts payable, purchased supplies and interacted with two Boards of Directors which included approximately 24 board members.

After having our daughter, Bethany, I chose to take a year off to raise her and our older boys, Marcus, Matthew, and Michael. It was great being a stay-at-home mom for the first time since having children. It was also the hardest job I've ever had!

One day my daughter and I were visiting my mother while the boys were in school. I was reading the newspaper and came across an advertisement for an opening for an Executive Assistant. As I read through the description and requirements, I knew I was qualified for the position and could do well. I had the right type of experience. I had managed an office, developed, implemented, and managed budgets, worked with Boards of Directors, created meeting minutes, managed payroll, completed and submitted quarterly tax returns, purchased supplies, and had a host of other experience as well.

"Success doesn't come to you,
you go to it."

**–MARVA COLLINS**

Several people asked me, "Why do you think you can do that job?" It wasn't that they didn't believe in me. It was more about the belief they had or didn't have in themselves. When they heard the title, Executive Assistant, they thought of an executive office and were uncomfortable seeing themselves in that world. Even though others doubted, I wasn't hesitant, or afraid of the environment and didn't accept their statements as a lack of belief in my ability.

# Luck is where preparedness and opportunity meet.

My first step was to prepare. This was long before the world of Internet technology and obtaining research at your fingertips. The name of the company was listed in the advertisement. I was familiar with the type of business they were in and the company name. However, I didn't have a lot of information, so I began asking my friends and relatives what they thought of the company as a way to determine if the company had a good reputation. What I learned intrigued me and kept my interest.

When you are considering a new position, discover everything you can about the company. Become a detective and make it your business to find out everything you can to determine if you want to be associated with the organization. I recommend you take full advantage of the internet and do multiple searches on line. Find out their mission and vision statements. Get familiar with their leadership team and Board of Directors. Read through financial reports to find out about their growth and market stability. Look to see if their values are prominently featured on their web pages or in their buildings. Notice what type of messaging they use in their marketing materials. Find out what non-profit organizations they support.

Before applying you need to know why you want to work for the company. Finding out these things after you are hired is too late. Being prepared is a key component to ace your interview.

After you've done your research about the company, create a list of questions you want to ask during your interview. These questions should include anything you weren't able to find out through your research, as well as specific questions about the position. Realize, you are a key hire for their company and you are interviewing them to determine if you want to join their team. Ask open-ended questions to create dialogue. Some key questions to consider are:

1. What can you tell me about your company values and how they are demonstrated?

2. How would you describe your company culture?

3. What are some of your short term and long term goals for the company and for this position?

4. What is a typical day in this position?

5. What did the last person in this position do well?

6. How do you describe an ideal candidate for
   this position?

My next step to preparing was to update my resume. I took one look at my existing resume and knew it was time to make several updates. To do so, I read through the job opening again and highlighted the requirements listed. Then I looked at each of my past positions and made sure every requirement where I had experience was accurately listed on my resume. I used clear and concise communication to make it easy for the person reviewing my resume to see the experience I had was relevant to what they were seeking.

# Why would I hire you?

I knew the competition would be tough and I wanted to stand out. If there was someone else as qualified as me, I wanted to win out. To do so, I needed to be better prepared than my competition. I put myself in my future manager's shoes and asked myself, "Why would I hire you?"

To create my "wow factor," I identified my past successes at each company where I had worked. I considered my performance reviews and praise I had received. I thought about moments of recognition. I carefully recalled times where I had saved the company money or created a process improvement.

After creating my list of past successes, I prepared for the interview by determining my top five selling points. I included these in my cover letter. I made it easy for my future employer to answer the question, "Why would I hire you?" And it worked! Every time I've used this method, I have received a job offer. Every time!

I considered who to list as references to assure my future employer of my character, trustworthiness, and integrity. I used past co-workers, managers, and friends involved in the community.

If you happen to know someone who works at the hiring organization, it's always a great idea to include him/her as a reference. To assure my references would be an advantage point for me and not be caught off guard or surprised, I called them ahead of time. I let them know about the position I was applying for and how my experience was relevant. I asked them if they were familiar with the company or knew anyone who worked for the organization. I asked if I could list them as references. Looking back, I've never had anyone decline my request. Instead, they thanked me for asking them ahead of time to be a reference and wished me good luck.

The research and mental preparation was complete. My resume was updated and fresh copies printed. My list of references was updated with names, addresses, and phone numbers. My cover letter was complete, featuring my top five selling points in bullet form in the middle section of the letter. I put my resume, list of references and cover letter inside sheet protectors and inserted the documents into a thin notebook. It looked sharp and professional.

It was now time to determine what I should wear. Where I was applying was a "corporate" type of environment with an "executive" feel, which meant I needed to dress the part. I needed to show up looking like I belonged there and was already part of the team. I looked through my closet and found the perfect outfit.

I asked my mother to watch my daughter and off I went to apply in person, as was requested. I told my mom I should only be a few minutes. Instead, I was gone for two hours! I showed up in a black suit, a colorful scarf that was knotted and tucked into the neckline of my suit so only a portion was showing. My makeup, hair, and perfume were conservative and not overdone. My nails were clean, freshly filed, and polished. I wore hose, simple gold studded earrings, a watch, and pumps… and carried a briefcase. My clothing was pressed and my shoes were shined. I located the receptionist, introduced myself, and told her I was there to drop off my resume and complete an application. She handed me the application and I provided her my resume.

Before I had completed the application, a supervisor approached me and asked if I had time for an interview. I was surprised and excited. She escorted me upstairs to the Executive Suite and I was interviewed by the Human Resource Director. I approached the Human Resource Director with a smile and an outstretched hand, shook her hand, and introduced myself. I noticed paperwork was piled high on her desk. She mentioned she had been filling in for the open position as well as doing her job and was really hoping to find the right candidate soon.

She began asking me questions about my skill set, experience, and background. I was able to answer her questions quickly, concisely, and confidently. The interview was going well and we were connecting on many levels regarding our interests and commonalties. As I shared my capabilities, I could see her physically relax. I remember saying, "I wish I could get started today so I could help you with some of the work on your desk." We both laughed. Then she said, with an exhausted sigh, "I would love that!"

She asked if I had time to stay to interview with the President or Vice-President. I told her I could do so. She left the office to see if either was available. I could feel my excitement building as I knew the interview had gone well enough to get through the first and second screenings. I was now on my way to the decision makers. I was glad I had a few extra notebooks with me with copies of my resume, list of references, and cover letter.

She came back and said the President wasn't available; however the Vice-President was available, and escorted me to his office. This was the first time I had interviewed with anyone of this status. I felt a little intimidated, nervous, and excited all rolled into one. I took a few deep breaths and grounded myself. I told myself this office wasn't much different than offices I had worked in before. Sure, it was in an Executive Suite and everyone was wearing suits but underneath it all, the work was similar. It was time to trust in my experience and capabilities and display confidence.

The interview went well. I was able to confidently and calmly answer his questions. Once the formality of the interview questions had come to a close and I started asking questions, I could sense he was impressed. All-in-all, the entire interview went really well.

He walked me back to the Human Resource Director's office. She told me she would be contacting me soon, thanked me for my time, and was very polite. I left feeling confident, knowing I had prepared and was able to deliver.

I went to my mom's to get my daughter and tell my mom about the experience. She was so excited to hear that I had not only dropped off my resume and completed the application, but also had the opportunity to interview with the Human Resource Director and Vice- President. She encouraged me and said with a laugh, "I hope you're ready to go back to work!"

Later that evening, I wrote handwritten thank you notes to the Human Resource Director and the Vice-President. I mailed them the next morning.

Within a few days, I received a phone call offering me the position! They told me over the phone their offer regarding salary and the benefit package. I tried to keep my excitement under control as I asked to meet with them in person to discuss the offer. *It's best to negotiate in person and not to accept the first offer provided.*

We agreed to meet the following day. I was familiar with salaries in our area and knew what was fair and reasonable based on my experience and the market place. I was also interested in at least two weeks' vacation time as well as the typical benefit package of health care, short and long term disability, retirement pension and 401K.

> "If you don't go after what you want, you'll never have it. If you don't ask, the answer is always no. If you don't step forward, you're always in the same spot."
>
> **–NORA ROBERTS**

During the negotiation, the Vice-President asked, "What is it going to take to get you to say yes?" I took a heavy sigh, and said a number $10,000 more than I had ever received. I was a bit hesitant to say the number out loud as I had never been paid that high of a salary before. I learned once an offer is presented, not to say another word until the other person speaks. Neither of us spoke for what seemed like an hour! In reality, it was probably no more than a few minutes. He broke the silence and said it was about $1,000 higher than he planned and would talk to Human Resources. I was beyond belief excited!

We then discussed the remaining benefits and everything fell into place. I was able to negotiate a high salary, three weeks vacation, health insurance package, short and long term disability, flexible working schedule, 401K and a pension!

I was pleased with the outcome and asked to secure the offer in writing once approved through Human Resources. I received a call the next day with everything approved and with the written offer. I told them I would like to sleep on it and would respond in the morning.

The next morning I called and accepted the offer and the rest is history! I secured my first Executive Assistant position and was ready to show everyone what I was capable of doing.

Years later, I was working at a different company and talking with a co-worker when she realized she had interviewed for this same position and wasn't selected. I remember her looking at me and saying, "You're the one who beat me out!" I was shocked I had been selected over her as she was sharp and professional and overall really impressive.

# Never discount the value of being prepared!
# It will give you the edge over another equally qualified candidate.

I've had a few other experiences I want you to know about because if they happened to me, they can happen to you, too. Have you ever been recruited? The only thing better than getting an offer for a job you really want is being recruited for a job that you might really like to have. This has happened to me twice and both times I was glad I took them up on their offers to apply for the position.

Each time I was recruited, it was completely out of the blue. I was working for a company and in a position I was proud of and wasn't looking for another job. I came home one day and had a message on my answering machine from a voice I didn't recognize. He explained his wife knew me and he was a Vice-President for a local company. He stated he was looking for an Executive Assistant and his wife told him, "You need Peggy!" What a great compliment and a huge surprise. I was intrigued.

I called him back and he explained the situation. He asked me to please consider applying because he'd really like to interview me. When I asked why he wanted me to apply, he explained that based on what he had heard, I had the exact skill set he was looking for. He said he had previous EA's and they were successful. This time, he was looking for someone with more than the basic EA skills. He wanted someone technically competent, but, more importantly, someone with strong interpersonal skills to create a collaborative and positive team dynamic. Again, I was intrigued, so I applied.

It ended up being a perfect match for me to utilize all I had learned and put into application. It was difficult to leave my current employer, as I highly valued my team, had learned a great deal from them, and believed in the work we were doing. However, I chose to leave because I wanted to say yes to the bigger opportunity.

> ## When you decide to leave a position, leave because you want to say yes to a new opportunity, not because you are running away from something.

The wife I mentioned earlier had worked with me several years prior. Thankfully, I made a positive impression on her and she remembered me. The thing she still speaks about today is the way I helped her succeed and made her feel welcomed when she first joined the company.

# People may not remember what you said, but they will always remember how you made them feel.

Once, during a negotiation, the recruiter and I were talking about the salary and benefit package and I had asked for more vacation than they were offering. He said, "This isn't something I can easily make happen." I asked, "What do you mean?" He said, "I would have to ask the Human Resource Director to write a letter to the regulatory agency asking for approval." I responded, "How long will that take?" He got the message and made it happen.

If you don't go after what you want, you'll never have it. You will rarely receive what you don't ask for. If you negotiate in a professional, reasonable, polite, and confident manner, you will be taken seriously and more often than not, you'll get what you ask for. You have to ask for what you want in life and know you are worth it!

To recap, if you want to ace your next interview, use my approach. This method has worked for me every time and I'm confident it will work for you!

**Prepare**: Read the job postings carefully to determine what you are interested in as well as the qualifications.

**Research**: Find out all you can about the company including its vision, mission, values, leadership team, financial standing, market presence and marketing approach. Determine if you are aligned with the company and the people who work for the company. I've interviewed a lot of people over the years and more often than not, this is the step people miss and, ultimately, fall short.

You need to make sure you really want to work for a company before you apply.

**Update your resume:** Align your resume to the current position. Make it easy for future employers to see your qualifications meet their standards. Use the key words utilized in the job posting.

**Determine your top five selling points**. You are there to represent yourself and make sure they walk away with the "Why should they hire you?" question clearly answered.

**Top selling points typically include:**

1. How you've made or saved the company money.
2. What you've done to improve processes and/or enhance performance.
3. How you created employee engagement.
4. Where you have shown leadership.

**Create a cover letter:** Emphasize your top five selling points. Weave these points into the interview by answering questions and talking about your background. The questions asked may not seem like a direct correlation to your top five selling points, however, with creativity you can give them two answers to one question.

**Update references:** Call references in advance to inform them you are applying for a new position. Ask for their support so your references will be used to your advantage.

**Suit Up:** Dress for the position you want. Look like the people who are interviewing you for the position. Bring documents with you for reference so you can easily answer questions. No need to sit in front of a blank table and feel you are being tortured by asking questions. Instead bring your tools, just as you would in an actual work setting. This is a way for you to demonstrate how you would work for their company.

**Ask Questions:** Interview the company by developing questions to ask in the interview. Whatever you could not find out about the company through your research, find out in the interview. Ask open-ended questions to create dialogue. Find out how their values are demonstrated in the workplace, what short term and long term goals are on the horizon, what their greatest challenges are, and how they describe the culture.

**Follow Up**: Write handwritten thank you notes to those who interviewed you. During the interview ask for a business card from those you meet. This will serve you well.

**Negotiate in Person:** A top executive would never negotiate over the phone. In person is best. Be polite, professional, firm, reasonable, and confident.

**Get offer in writing:** Don't leave anything to chance or to someone's memory. Make sure everything is documented.

**Thank you:** Follow up with another handwritten thank you note to your future employer.

You miss 100% of the shots you don't take.

**–WAYNE GRETZKY**

# Powerful Partnerships

"Coming together is a beginning;
keeping together is progress;
working together is success."

**–HENRY FORD**

CHAPTER**SIX**

# Powerful Partnerships

One of my most successful partnerships is with my loving husband, René. We've been blessed with a marriage that has withstood the test of time for 29 years. Our greatest blessings are our four amazing children, our fabulous daughters-in-law, and our incredible grandchildren. René and I have been together longer than we've been apart and I can't imagine our lives without one another. There is nothing I treasure more than my family.

My husband is my best example of what it means to have a successful partnership. When you've been together for nearly thirty years, trust me, you've seen some incredibly human and vulnerable moments. We've been there for each other through the good times and the bad. We've seen each other at our best and our worst. There have been times when we felt the only person we had in our corner was the other one, and at that moment, the only thing we needed was each other. In fact, when we were married, we didn't have a lot of people in our corner and our theme song was, "Ain't no stopping us now" by Brothers Johnson. To this day, when we hear that song, it still brings a smile to our faces because we knew then what we know now…if we have each other everything else is going to be alright.

Ironically, many of the same factors that create a successful marriage are the same factors that create a successful business partnership. First, and foremost, it takes trust. Without trust, there is no foundation. Secondly, you must realize you are better together than you are apart and you rely on one another for your success. Thirdly, when you go through a challenge together and help each other get through it; your bond becomes stronger than ever.

No matter how great your current partnership is with your executive, there is always room to improve. When you understand how impactful a powerful partnership is on your career, you'll be motivated to learn how to manage the relationship to get the highest possible return.

## WHAT IS A SYNERGISTIC PARTNERSHIP?

The first time I experienced a synergistic relationship was with a Vice-President. The partnership started out with him recruiting me, which is a pretty fantastic way to start. He told me had an opening for an Executive Assistant and I was the perfect person for the position. He told me my strength in leading teams, my professionalism, and interpersonal skills were exactly what he needed. He made me feel very valuable. He had a clear goal and purpose for me. He also gave me complete authority and freedom to act. He valued my opinions and thought of me as a professional, a leader, and a partner. We became a united team and mutually respected and trusted one another. Our goals and values were aligned, and our styles complimented each other. We experienced successes and overcame challenges together, and we mutually enjoyed working with one another. This is the type of partnership every assistant should have the opportunity to experience!

I want you to experience what it is like to:

1. Feel valued and respected.

2. Have a clear goal and purpose.

3. Have authority and freedom to act.

4. Be thought of and treated as a professional, a leader, and a business partner.

5. Be part of a united team and have your goals aligned with your executive.

The definition of a synergistic partnership is when the result is greater than the sum of their individual effects or capabilities. To me, synergy is where the result of the efforts of two or more people is greater than individual results. Synergy is the ability of a group to outperform even its best individual member. A synergistic partnership may be difficult to express, however, when you experience synergy, you feel it before you can see it or describe it. Whether you are the executive or the administrative assistant, once you experience a synergistic partnership, you'll never want to settle for anything less.

There are many benefits to having a strong partnership, some benefits are:

1. Empowerment

2. Increased productivity

3. Less relationship management

4. Trust and communication

5. Shared values

6. Common goals

7. Getting each other to give his or her best for the benefit of the partnership

8. Bringing out the best in each other

9. Humor

10. Fun

11. Celebration

12. Camaraderie

## DEVELOPING THE PARTNERSHIP

There are three basic ways to develop a partnership:

1. Understand who the partners are and their styles.

2. Understand their roles and priorities.

3. Establish routine communication.

I've worked for a variety of manager's who were as diverse as you can possibly imagine. They each had their own unique style and way of doing business. Each had his or her strengths and weaknesses, as well as quirks and hot buttons. It would be a mistake to assume all executives would want to manage their offices the same. You'll need to ask some strategic and critical questions in order to find out everything you need to know about your executive. The key is to learn as much as you can. Think about it this way, how can you support someone you don't know?

## SETTING THE FOUNDATION

During your first week, find out how your manager prefers the office and the workload to be managed. While asking questions, offer your office management experience by providing suggestions. Working together, determine the best method for managing your office.

Here are a few of the questions you'll want to ask:

1. Would you like an open door policy? Or, would you appreciate the role of a gatekeeper to limit and/or screen the drop by visits?

2. Are you a morning or afternoon person? What time do you usually arrive at the office and leave the office?

3. Would you like me to answer your phone or would you prefer to do so? Would you like me to screen your calls? Are there certain callers who you want to get through no matter if you are in a meeting or otherwise busy when they call?

4. Is there a preferred time for a daily meeting? Would you like to have it at the beginning of the day or the end of the day?

5. When is the best time to approach you regarding a sensitive subject?

6. When is the best time to schedule high level meetings?

7. What are your pet peeves and quirks?

8. What are your expectations regarding how email, voicemail, and incoming mail are handled?

9. What is your expectation regarding tracking deliverables?

10. What are your expectations regarding how the administrative assistant acts independently and on behalf of the executive?

## MOVING PAST THE BASICS

Once these basic questions are answered, you can move past the basic partnership level by finding out what's important to your executive. Talk to him/her about roles and priorities. Let it be known you want to do all you can to help create success. Ask for a copy of his/her goals and have a conversation with him/her centered on those goals. Align your goals to those goals.

Find out what your manager thinks and worries about. To assure your manager's success, you need to know what your manager is accountable for and what is measured. Once you have this information, find a way to help your manager deliver! I promise you, if you help your manager reach one of his/her goals, he/she will value you tremendously.

These are strategic questions to help you form your partnership. With answers to these questions, you'll be aligned with your executive and be able to manage the day-to-day operations. You will also be able to increase your level of interaction with his/her direct reports and earn his/her respect because he/she will know you are in the know at a strategic level. You'll be armed with information that will provide insights and judgments which will help you determine what actions to take and when, as well as how to manage your executive's time, calendar, and priorities.

## COMMUNICATION IS KEY

Communication is essential in developing a powerful partnership. Communicate clearly, openly, and often. You can communicate in person, email, text, written notes, or whatever medium works best for the given situation. All the executives I have worked for have stated the hardest part of their jobs is communication. There is a huge amount of information coming into an executive's office. Decisions are made based on that information and then information is shared. Often the information needs to be massaged before it can be shared. The political landscape needs to be considered. Together, you and your executive need to determine who will need what level of information and what background needs to be provided with the information. Your ability to handle the communication on behalf of your executive is worth its weight in gold! This is an area where you can really save your executive time. When you master this area, you'll be able to draft messages on behalf of your manager, before you and your executive even discuss what messages are needed. Over time, your executive will defer to you to handle those messages.

Most of us support very busy people. Because of this, it is imperative you don't leave the daily meeting with your manager to chance. Instead, schedule time with your manager. As administrative assistants, we control our manager's calendars. It is our job to make our managers more effective and more successful than they could be without the support of an administrative assistant. Your meeting with your manager is crucial to his/her success because you are managing the executive's calendar, triaging email, tracking deliverables, obtaining information to prepare your executive for meetings, gathering and writing talking points and getting all the details about upcoming events. When you meet with your executive, make the best use of his/her time by being thoroughly prepared and having all the information you need at your fingertips so you can quickly and concisely answer any question he/she may have. To do so, you must be in the know and have an understanding of what is happening today, tomorrow, and in the future.

I've heard administrative assistants say their managers don't want to meet with them and don't see value in the daily meeting. I'm always perplexed because I've never had a manager say this to me. I know, without any doubt, the information I give to my manager in the daily meeting isn't provided in any other meeting. My manager could likely obtain a portion of the information I provide, if he wasn't in meetings for most of the day, which is why triaging email is such a key part of the role of the administrative assistant. I know I am saving him time and he knows it as well. Our managers are often in meetings and haven't had time to review email the entire day. When we meet with our managers and alert them about emails, deliverable due dates, and gather information based on upcoming meetings, we save them time. Demonstrate your value by making it your mission to save your managers time and facilitate their success.

Most days I have a long list of things I need to discuss with my executive. I arrange items in priority order to assure what I must cover, gets covered. I pay close attention to my executive to make sure he's still "present" and hasn't drifted off because of the many obligations on his plate. If I feel he's "checked out" and is no longer able to take in the information or have the discussion regarding the things on my list, I pause and state, "That's it for today. The rest can wait until tomorrow." Every once in a while, he will urge me to continue reviewing the remaining material. Most of the time, he says, "Thank you. You know me too well."

Playing the role of an advisor is another key role of an administrative assistant. I've learned to allow room to discuss what my executive would like to cover, instead of only being focused on my list of "to do's." Often, when I ask him how things are going, or what's on his mind, he'll open up and share something with me he wants to discuss. It's during these times the administrative assistant becomes the advisor and a stronger partnership develops. The door is opened to a deeper level of dialogue and brainstorming begins as the executive asks for advice regarding an approach or an idea he /she is considering. This sharing of ideas allows your executive to see how well you know the organization and all the players. When you help your executive see another view point and offer another approach, it helps the executive consider many other aspects of a given situation. These are the types of conversations where trust is paramount as well as the ability to hold information in confidence. This interaction defines what it means to work "with" someone versus working "for" someone. When this happens, you have moved from the typical administrative assistant role into the role of a business partner.

One of the best ways to help your executive is to use the art of strategic questioning. For instance, your executive has agreed to provide a presentation to someone who isn't directly tied to his/her priorities. By agreeing to this activity, his/her schedule is now tied up and no longer available for something more strategic that does align with priorities. You can guide your executive back to what is most important to him/her by asking strategic questions, such as: "I realize you agreed to provide a presentation to ABC Group. Help me understand how this fits into the big picture and relates to your goals and priorities." When you use strategic questioning effectively, your executive will be guided back to what is really important.

Once you experience this level of partnership, you realize what a powerful role you have as an executive assistant. It is essential for administrative assistants to realize the power they have and respect the power as well. If you misuse the power, you'll likely only have the opportunity to do so briefly before your executive knows it and that opportunity will come to a screeching halt! Administrative assistants are in key positions to influence our executives. Many times, we are their advisors, confidants and encouragers. We hold them in the palm of our hands. We can use this power to encourage them and pull them forward to greater success, or we can misuse our power for our own agenda. When you respect the power you have and understand your job is to help others be more successful with you than they are without you, you'll be respecting the power appropriately. Respect and realize the powerful role you have! I hope you re-read this paragraph and embrace it.

## UNDERSTANDING YOUR PARTNER'S STYLE

In order to partner well with others, you need to know their personality styles. Life would be easier if we all communicated the same and had the same thinking patterns. However, that is certainly not the case. We each have our preferred method of communication and due to these differences can find ourselves in the middle of a conversation or a meeting where the communication just isn't working.

Interestingly, our behaviors are predictable. The way we interact with others...our preferred method for communicating becomes a habit. We have probably used the same method since we were very young and have developed a pattern in our interactions with others. Sure, we've matured and have a different vocabulary. Most of us have learned we can't throw a fit and get away with it.

Mankind has been studying variations of four basic behavior patterns for 2500 years! Hippocrates identified four basic temperaments in 460BC. In the 1920's, Carl Jung developed a concept he called the intuitor, thinker, feeler, and sensor, which are the foundation for the Meyers-Briggs Type indicator.

There are many interpersonal style models available. I've learned several: Meyers-Briggs, Social Styles, Colors, Animals, DISC, and more. Most interpersonal profile testing uses a model with four quadrants to describe the various styles. Through all the books I've read and all the research I've done, I've learned no style is better than another and most people have the ability to express elements of all four styles. The question that always comes up when I do interpersonal style training is, "What is the best style for an administrative assistant?" Again, there is not one best style. No matter what your preferred style, you can be successful as an administrative assistant. It's important to note these interpersonal style profiles indicate your preferred communication style, not your communication capabilities.

Personality type assessments can be extremely costly and complicated, so I decided to create my own based on the various models I've researched and applied. My model is very simplistic, easy-to-use and understand, and easy to remember!

Here's my Personality Profile Model. Notice each quadrant has a picture which illustrates the style as well as a strength and a limitation. This allows you to quickly glance at the model and recognize each style.

The more you know about your style and that of your executive, the more likely you will be able to form a powerful partnership. I encourage you to study your executive's behaviors and communication style. Observe how he/she interacts with others. Find out if he/she is prone to focusing on "people" or on "tasks." Recognize how he/she speaks. Does he/she speak in terms of "telling" or "asking?" Make it your mission to know what makes your executive tick.

I'll provide you a little insight into each of these styles through the strengths and limitations summary below. The best way to experience this information is through a workshop which includes a personality profile assessment and applied learning activities. This workshop is consistently one of my attendee's favorite sessions.

## Strengths/Limitations Summary

| Enthusiastic / Overbearing | Goal-Oriented / Distant | Personable / Timid | Thorough / Perfectionist |
|---|---|---|---|
| Strengths | Strengths | Strengths | Strengths |
| • Risk Taker<br>• Inspiring<br>• Open and Direct<br>• Pursues Change<br>• Socially Skilled<br>• Persuasive<br>• Competitive<br>• Confident | • Practical<br>• Orderly<br>• Very Direct<br>• Self-Determined<br>• Organized<br>• Traditional<br>• Goal-Oriented<br>• Dependable | • Team-Oriented<br>• Caring<br>• Devoted<br>• Sensitive<br>• Enthusiastic<br>• Helpful<br>• Accessible | • Exacting<br>• Meticulous<br>• Practical<br>• Thorough<br>• Factual<br>• Reserved<br>• Calm<br>• Has High Standards |
| Limitations | Limitations | Limitations | Limitations |
| • Impatient<br>• Manipulative<br>• Pushy<br>• Intimidating<br>• Overbearing<br>• Restless<br>• Abrasive<br>• Reactive | • Rigid<br>• Unapproachable<br>• Distant<br>• Dogmatic<br>• Stubborn<br>• Critical<br>• Insensitive | • Impractical<br>• Vulnerable<br>• Hesitant<br>• Too Other-Oriented<br>• Indecisive<br>• Subjective | • Withdrawn<br>• Perfectionist<br>• Passive<br>• Slow to Get Things Done<br>• Dull<br>• Sullen<br>• Shy |

Throughout my career, I've worked for all different types of managers. Some were easier to work with than others. Some were pretty difficult. No matter what the situation was, I learned from each of them and am grateful for the experience.

Some of the managers I've worked for were so goal-oriented, it was as if they had blinders on and couldn't see anything else but the goal. I remember one executive who didn't even realize one of his direct reports was pregnant until she was out on maternity leave! I've also worked for a manager who didn't recognize the importance of thanking the staff, so I took on the task of telling staff thank you for the work they had done. It wasn't that he didn't appreciate the work that had been completed; he simply didn't feel the need to thank staff for doing what they were hired to do.

One of the best things you can do for your executive is to fill the gap. Know your manager's strengths and limitations so well that you set him/her up for success by utilizing your strengths to fill the gap in one of the areas of weakness. For example, if your executive is an Enthusiastic/Overbearing type of individual and is so excited about a particular topic that he/she doesn't allow for others on the team to talk, provide him/her feedback and make a suggestion.

> *"Mr. Executive, when we were in the meeting earlier today and you were so excited to share the news about the XYZ project, I made a few observations I'd like to share with you. I saw Mr. Direct Report trying to make a comment, did you notice him? I've noticed when you get excited about some-thing, sometimes it makes it difficult for anyone else to talk. Would you like me to give you a signal in the future to help you allow for staff to make a comment?"*

I've used this technique before and it works well when your executive knows you are doing all you can to assure he/she is successful.

If you don't possess the strength your executive needs in a particular situation, team him/her up with someone who does.

This type of partnership won't happen overnight. Some partnerships form quicker than others, some partnerships are better than others. All powerful partnerships take effort and time. It takes time to develop, time to build, and time to maintain a partnership.

## ADAPT TO THEIR STYLE

In our roles as administrative assistants, we need to be flexible, nimble and highly adaptable to our environments and those whom we support. When I ask executives, "What is the most important skill in the role of the executive assistant?" The most common response is, "Flexibility."

> # Blessed are the flexible, for they shall not be bent out of shape!

In one of my workshops, we were discussing flexibility. One of the attendees said flexibility is one of the four corner stones for having a successful administrative career. He laughed and said he wasn't sure what the other three corner stones were, but he knew flexibility holds up all the rest! You can be the most competent administrative assistant on the planet and if you aren't flexible, you will not be successful.

## WHEN STYLES CLASH

Frustrations often come when we work with someone in an opposite quadrant from our quadrant. For example: The "Enthusiastic / Overbearing" who has a tendency to be pushy, expressive, likes risk and change – compared to the "Thorough / Perfectionist" who likes consistency and the status quo, is reserved, and dislikes aggressiveness. Imagine the natural clash with these two communication styles. At the core, these communication styles are complete opposites. The way each of these styles prefers to communicate instantly rubs the other style the wrong way.

When you are in this situation, you'll probably notice a shift in the energy between you and the other person. You can feel the invisible wall come up and the communication is stifled. You may even notice the negative energy before either of you speak, because we communicate with more than words. Our personality and communication style is expressed in our body language as well as in our verbal communication.

If you find yourself in this situation, I have a few tips for you:

**Dial your style down**. When you notice you aren't communicating effectively, use your self-awareness skills to determine if you are coming across too engrained in your own style for the other person to relate to you. For example, if you are an "Enthusiastic / Overbearing" type and you are talking with a "Thorough / Perfectionist," you may be too animated and too expressive for his level of comfort. By "dialing down" your preferred enthusiastic approach, you'll find the tension begin to ease and communication begin.

**Genuinely appreciate your differences**. When you have a better awareness of the diverse styles, you'll understand how each style contributes to the success of the team. Once you internalize the fact there is no right or wrong style, and no style is better than another, you will be more apt to truly appreciate all styles.

Learn as much as you can about your style and the style of your executive. Knowing more about yourself will help you be more flexible so you can deal effectively with your executive and put your unique traits to work for you, instead of against you.

**Mirror their style**. When people perceive you to be like them, they are more comfortable talking to you. When you mirror others, you are a reflection of them. If they are standing, stand. If they are seated, sit. If they are smiling, smile. If they are reserved, be reserved. Use their same behaviors. Use the same rate of speech and posture. This makes the other person feel comfortable because he/she perceives you to be like him/her, which enables communication. This is not to say I'm advising you to be fake; it simply means to modify your communication style to allow your communication to be more effective.

When you use these methods, you are speaking their language which allows others to hear you and understand you. This does not mean you need to change and become someone else. It simply means, in order to communicate more effectively and develop a powerful partnership; you may need to make some adjustments to your preferred method of communication.

## Maintaining the Partnership

Once you've established the partnership, you'll need to continue to nurture it. You can nurture the partnership in a number of ways. By performing at your optimum level and doing so consistently, your executive will know he can trust you to perform and can relax, knowing you've got all the details handled.

Another key aspect in maintaining the partnership is keeping confidential information held in confidence. Doing so builds trust. When your executive trusts you as a confidant and as a high performer, you've got the foundation for a powerful partnership.

Show recognition to your executive for a job well done. The saying, "It's lonely at the top" is very true. I've learned that most executives appreciate being cared about as a person, not just as an executive. Demonstrate compassion for the difficulty of the position and the weight upon their shoulders. Most executives aren't recognized or thanked often enough, especially in light of everything they do. Make a point of finding ways to genuinely recognize your executive when she has done a great job.

Emulate a strong professional code by being known as someone who under promises and over delivers. Do 10% more than what is required, requested, or expected. One of the essential elements of a powerful partnership is accountability and follow through. What happens to a relationship when someone doesn't follow up? What about the opposite? What happens when someone delivers quicker than expected and with more information than requested? The latter is the behavior you want to emulate. Most of us don't want to work with a "whiner" or a "can't happen" kind of person. In fact, we avoid these types of people. Be known as the one who always follows through, is dependable, reliable and accountable.

# Mirror your partner's dreams; the relationship will grow.

**Collaborate with others and help others succeed.** The serendipitous part about this is that it will build your self-respect and confidence. Help people find a way to get things done.

**Lead by example.** You and your executive are a team which means you both must "walk the walk" and "talk the talk." When you are working for the manager who is making the decisions, you no longer have the right to blame management. You are a team and you both need to support one another. Be the person you want to look up to.

## THE POWER OF FEEDBACK

When you work with someone closely day after day, you will be in a situation where you need to provide feedback. The situation might be as small as telling your executive he has a dirty nose before walking into an All Staff meeting. These types of feedback conversations may be uncomfortable and awkward but fairly easy to do. Your executive will appreciate the kind approach and will know you had his back and saved him from an embarrassing situation.

There will be other times when the situation is much more impactful and can be highly political. These conversations are downright scary. This is where the trust you developed early on in the partnership will carry tremendous weight. Be confident and courageous enough to offer feedback and have the difficult conversations. The last thing your executive needs is another "yes" person. Executives need someone who they trust to tell them the truth. This isn't what they want to hear or what will make them feel better. These are the conversations that are designed to make your executive better. This takes guts, confidence, judgment and caring enough about your executive's success that you are willing to take the risk. I've had these types of conversations with executives and, every time, I was scared, yet each and every time my executive was grateful for the conversation and thanked me for my open and honest feedback.

Years ago, I learned a method for giving feedback called "SBI." This method will work for giving feedback up, down, and across the organization.

**S** = Situation

**B** = Behavior

**I** = Impact

Close with message

For example: You have someone on your team who is disruptive in meetings. He is having side bar conversations and interrupting the meeting. Here's how to handle it.

**S**ituation: "In our meeting earlier today."

**B**ehavior: "I noticed you were having side bar conversations."

**I**mpact: "This behavior interrupted our meeting. The team lost focus on the topic and confusion followed."

Message: "In the future, please keep side bar conversations to a minimum, so our meetings will be more productive. Will you do that for me and the team?"

When receiving feedback, first and foremost, assume the person providing feedback has positive intent and cares enough about you to help you succeed.

1. **Listen** with an open heart and open mind. It might not be warranted, but you won't get far without it.

2. **Ask questions** and assume the message comes from a place of goodwill and generosity. Skepticism doesn't help you hear.

3.  **Reflect** on the message and consult a mentor to help process the information and determine changes you may make.

## SETTING BOUNDARIES

When you've had a powerful partnership with an executive, it can be difficult to know the importance of setting boundaries. One way to assure you don't cross the line is to treat him/her with respect and dignity, always remembering your manager is your boss. Be careful about becoming too familiar and too casual with the person you support.

When I was first starting out as an executive assistant, I didn't understand this as well as I do now. There are some situations I wouldn't advise, such as having a drink alone with your manager. If your job requires you to travel with your manager, setting boundaries is even more important. The best way for me to say this is bluntly: Do not put yourself or your manager in a compromising situation. Enough said.

## WHAT IF THE PARTNERSHIP ISN'T WORKING?

If you find yourself in a situation where the partnership isn't happening, the first step is to assess the partnership and identify what isn't working. Focus on the facts and remain objective as you ask yourself these questions. Do your best to avoid becoming emotional.

1.  Where are the gaps?

2.  Where are the challenges?

3.  Where are the strengths?

4. Am I aware of his/her style and putting that knowledge to work in my day-to-day interactions?

5. What haven't I tried?

6. What's stopping me?

Now that you've assessed the facts about the state of the partnership, you are ready to create an improvement plan. This plan isn't only for partnerships that are broken; every partnership can benefit from an improvement plan which results in taking it to the next level.

## The Improvement Plan

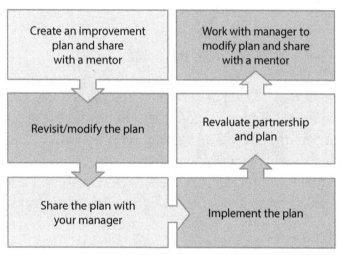

The first step is to schedule the meeting. Say something along the lines of: *"I scheduled a meeting for us to talk about how we manage the office. The meeting is scheduled for 1½ hours; however, it should only take us 45 minutes. I wanted us to have plenty of time to discuss this topic."*

Taking this action will demonstrate to your manager that you are actively engaged in creating a successful and productive partnership.

Walk through each of the steps in the Improvement Plan. Communicate professionally by discussing the facts and keep emotions in check. Talk about what is working, what could be improved upon, and together determine the next steps. Ask your manager for suggestions and offer your ideas. Keep the discussion focused on developing a highly efficient, productive environment.

> "Whenever you're in conflict with someone, there is one factor that can make the difference  between damaging your relationship and deepening it.
> That factor is attitude."
>
> **–WILLIAM JAMES**

The point of the meeting is to improve the partnership and to get buy in on a new approach, not to assign blame and rehash past issues to determine who was right and who was wrong. Keep your manager's style in mind. Don't take things personally if your manager isn't overly enthusiastic about the new plan and approach. Just be prepared to follow through with what is agreed upon.

If you've done all these steps and given it enough time to change, it might be time to seek a new partnership. If this is the case, know that:

1. The partnership failed. This doesn't mean you failed.

2. Because you took all the right steps and invested time and effort into the relationship, you can leave without regrets.

3. You stayed professional along the journey of finding a new position and didn't burn any bridges.

Now, you can find a new position and exit gracefully.

Have I done this? Yes! Several years ago, I worked for a great company. I had a great job. I was successful, had increased responsibility, a growing salary, a change in job titles, and was doing really well except in one area. The CEO and I had a difference in values. Over time, I came to realize the CEO wasn't going to change his values, so I had two choices. I could stay and buy into those values or I could leave. I chose to leave and it was absolutely the right choice for me.

## POWERFUL PARTNERSHIP MEMORIES

I am so grateful for the powerful partnerships I've had throughout my career. I made a conscious decision to align my goals with my executive's goals and found ways to have our styles complement one another. It was my goal to become a united team with mutual respect and trust. I've had the opportunity to develop powerful partnerships and know without a doubt I made a difference in my executive's success.

> "Our success has really been based on partnerships from the very beginning."
>
> **—BILL GATES**

I can recall times when I was the chief confidant and advisor and together we figured a way through a challenging situation. I've helped brainstorm possible solutions and talked through all the details to arrive at a path forward. I've been able to remind my executive of a message he wanted to deliver, provided information at a key moment, and quickly wrote a note and quietly passed it during a meeting to help him share the information he wanted to share with his team, which not only helped my executive but helped the entire team.

Knowing I've made a difference is what keeps me going and contributing at a high level. This is especially true when you are working for the top executive. There is an entire organization depending on your executive to deliver so each of them remains gainfully employed. What a huge responsibility, and we, as administrative assistants, are part of that equation. We are often the ones holding everything together in the middle of a crisis or chaos.

## Never doubt what a key role you play as an administrative assistant.

I've been an administrative assistant for long enough I've not only experienced leaving a company, and having my executive leave, I've also experienced the death of an executive. One of the most humbling and respectful moments was when a past executive's wife asked me to speak at his funeral. We were in a simple back yard filled with friends and family. There were tears and laughter. A few members of the former core team spoke and shared humorous stories as well as paid our respects. Our stories defined his character and integrity. As each of us spoke, we realized his family wasn't aware of many things he had accomplished and overcome, in his role. We had worked together for several years and the stories were numerous. Watching his family and friends light up as the stories were told was a moment I will always cherish.

"The most important single ingredient
in the formula of success is the knack of
getting along with people."

**–THEODORE ROOSEVELT**

# You Are a Leader – Yes, You!

"Though leadership may be hard to define,
the one characteristic common to all leaders
is the ability to make things happen."

**–TED W. ENGSTROM**

CHAPTER**SEVEN**

# You Are a Leader – Yes, You!

## LEADING YOUR MANAGER

In the last chapter, we talked about the importance of managing your manager. Most of us don't think about managing our manager's calendar and deliverables as leading our manager. However, it's those tasks and a host of other things that a great administrative assistant does which, in fact, qualify as leading her manager. When we ask strategic questions to redirect our managers, we are leading our managers. When we encourage our managers to keep moving forward through a difficult challenge, we are leading our managers. When we provide information to our managers and they engage us in dialogue to share their ideas and possible paths forward and ask for our advice, we are leading our managers.

Experienced administrative assistants are experts at leading their managers and the beautiful thing is most managers don't even realize its happening. They just appreciate how smoothly things are running and the success they are experiencing.

Administrative assistants are leaders when they gracefully, tactfully, and respectfully lead their managers.

## LEADERSHIP IS NOT A TITLE

"Not your job title, but your job.
What do you do when you're doing your work?
What's difficult and important about what you do,
what change do you make, what do you do that's
hard to live without and worth paying for?"

"I change the people who stop at my desk,
from visitors to guests."

"I give my boss confidence."

"I close sales."

"If your job is "showing up,"
time to raise the stakes."

**–SETH GODIN**

Some of us are more comfortable in the role of leadership and nominate ourselves to leadership roles. Others consider themselves quiet leaders, leading from behind the scenes. Others have an attitude of servitude which means they lead through their service to others. No matter how you choose to lead, recognize administrative assistants are leaders.

I have worked with some outstanding administrative assistants; most did not consider themselves to be leaders. The reason most administrative assistants don't see themselves as leaders is because they support those who have leadership titles. Many administrative assistants aren't comfortable being in charge and don't want the accountability that goes along with the authority. However, when you think about what administrative assistants do in their day-to-day roles, it's easy to realize they are leaders.

I talked with an administrative assistant who shared with me she didn't think of herself as a leader. I was shocked she felt this way. Without question, I thought of her as a leader. I told her, "I think you are a leader and demonstrate leadership in your day-to-day interactions, through your example, the way you graciously teach others how to do new tasks, share how to find information, demonstrate a consistent high level of performance, keep a cool head under tremendous pressure and chaos, and so much more. All of these things are how you demonstrate leadership each and every day!" I could see her eyes begin to light up as she realized all the things I said were true. She thought she was "just" doing her job and didn't think of those behaviors as ways of expressing leadership.

One of my workshops is titled, "Taking your Career to the Next Level" and leadership is a huge component of the workshop. During the workshop, I have the attendees write down their definition of "leadership."

Leadership, as they have defined it, is a primary responsibility of any administrative assistant, meaning it continuously ranks among the top five things on which we spend our time, attention and resources.

After independently completing this exercise, the attendees then participate as groups at their tables and identify the key take aways. Here are the most common responses for the definition of leadership:

1. Good communication skills
2. Sharing Information
3. Understanding the needs of the group
4. Knowing team strengths and utilizing strengths
5. Good listening skills

6. Treating others with respect

7. Setting the example / Leading by example

8. Empowering others / Building others up

9. Motivating / Inspiring others

10. People skills / Interpersonal skills

11. Demonstrating emotional strength

12. Body language

13. Accountable

14. Resourceful – Have a Plan B

15. Adaptable and flexible

The best part of the class is the moment when the administrative assistants realize the way they have defined leadership describes themselves and their day-to-day environment and behaviors!

> "It's not your position that gives
> you power – it's your behavior."
>
> **–NAN RUSSELL**

Administrative assistants routinely share information and have learned how to communicate with respect, tact, and diplomacy. We often know the staff better than our manager does. Staff members share their thoughts and ideas and also vent to the administrative assistants in their work groups. Staff members tell their administrative assistants what is happening in their personal lives as well as what is happening in their work groups. Through these conversations, compiled with our observations and interactions, we learn about the group's needs, challenges, and strengths. We share this information with our managers and encourage our managers to utilize the strengths of the team as the opportunities arise. Administrative assistants are extremely resourceful, think ahead, and almost always have a Plan B. They are also flexible and adaptable enough to move with the flow and are prepared to act on Plan B, should Plan A fall apart.

## Administrative assistants are leaders and demonstrate the behaviors of leadership.

In Nan Russell's book, "The Titleless Leader," she defines a leader as: "An individual, who delivers results without title or authority, using common sense, but uncommonly displays best-of-self behavior that, when practiced, creates trust, influence, and followership. A self-chosen leadership style is available to anyone no matter the position or role."

John Maxwell, one of my favorite authors, has written several books on leadership. Here's one of his quotes:

> "Leaders develop daily, not in a day.
> It's human nature to overestimate the event and underestimate the process.
>
> We want instant results, but instead of focusing our attention on the end point, we would be wise to make the most of the present day."
>
> **–JOHN MAXWELL**

I've heard the "life is a journey, not a destination" quote many times. I always thought it sounded nice, but I never bought into the meaning of the message. I'm one of those "focus on the goal, get the achievement" types of people. I'm also very enthusiastic and passionate. Every time I'd try to wrap my head around this philosophy, I came up short. Then, one day, it hit me! You have to live life in your desired destination. You can't wait until you reach your desired destination to start living the life you want to live, AND you must enjoy the journey along the way. Otherwise, your life will be focused on delayed happiness. You'll be happy when you lose weight, when you get that new car or new home, when you finish writing your book. Say for example, your desired state is peace. To have a peaceful life, you must live a peaceful life. It seems pretty simple, right? You must live the life you want to have. You can't arrive at a peaceful life if you are living anything but peacefully. I finally got it!

I've wanted to write a book for years, so I had to begin living the life of a writer. This meant for me, I needed to make the conscious decision to focus my free time on writing. It also meant I had to give up other activities and be happy about that decision. Otherwise, I wouldn't be enjoying the journey of becoming a writer. If I feel I am sacrificing to become a writer and feel resentful about missing out on activities, the finished book won't have the same sweetness as desired. I must enjoy the process. This is what John is trying to tell us in the quote above. We must enjoy and not underestimate the process, for it is the process that molds us into becoming who and what we desire to be.

I believe deep down we all know we are leaders, however, our confidence doesn't always allow us to act upon our leadership instincts. We can change this by becoming more confident and knowing without any doubt that leadership is not a position or level of authority but is demonstrated through our behavior. We have every right to behave as leaders and, in fact, our managers and our organizations would benefit from each of us stepping up to leadership in a big way!

If you are doubtful you can be a leader without the title, consider the manager who leads only with his title and power of authority. Take a moment to picture this person. What comes to mind is someone who is egocentric and on a power trip, and someone who is clueless about his team and the environment. How effective is this person? Yet, he has all the power. People will do what he says because he is in charge, but they aren't motivated or inspired to do more than what is being directed. His team members don't feel valued or cared about and don't show loyalty or commitment. This type of leader's only leadership card is the power card. Take away his power and he has no leadership, influence, or followership.

Administrative assistants are often aware of new committees being formed to work on a focused area. Don't wait to be asked to join a committee. If you are interested in serving on a committee and have expertise and interest that would be beneficial to the committee, volunteer! You will grow by doing so and you'll help the committee reach a better outcome. I don't recall a time when my manager told me I couldn't be involved, nor do I recall a time when the committee didn't welcome my involvement. John Maxwell also says, "When you quit growing, you relinquish the privilege of leadership. You simply can't take others to a place you've never been yourself."

# Administrative assistants demonstrate leadership when we challenge ourselves to get out of our comfort zones and volunteer.

## LEADING A TEAM

In our role as administrative assistants, we are often tasked with leading a team of administrative assistants. This is a delicate dance, as we typically don't have direct authority to manage this group of assistants. Instead, we are asked to lead through influence, encouragement, and by sharing information and knowledge. It's a dotted line and a lot of grey area to manage. It's also a wonderful opportunity to put our leadership to work and help others.

I was so excited to lead my first group of administrative assistants. I had a lot of creative ideas and couldn't wait to get started. I wanted to make a difference and knew how powerful a group of administrative assistants could be. I knew we could make a huge impact. I had all of this knowledge and I couldn't wait to put it into action.

> "People care more about how much you care about them, than how much you know."
>
> **–CAVETT ROBERT**

I was, however, focused on the knowledge and not on the people on the team. Looking back, I realize I thought I had all the answers and wanted to share them, thinking the others would get excited and embrace the knowledge. What I didn't understand, at the time, was getting to know them as individuals was as important as knowing how to create a plan and a vision for our team.

I was leading a team of administrative assistants. Notice the key word here: **"I"** decided we should have team goals. So **"I"** created a huge slide deck and presented "our" goals to them. How do you think this went over? Not so good. Inside, I was devastated. I had spent a great deal of time creating our goals and I knew they were an outstanding set of goals. Why weren't they excited? Well, they weren't excited because those goals weren't "the team's" goals; they were what **"I"** had dictated as our goals.

> "More powerful than a push is the
> gentle magnetic pull of a big idea
> and a common purpose."
>
> **–WILFRED PETERSON**

## LEARNING ABOUT YOUR TEAM

I had to learn to manage my expectations and be flexible. When we "tell" people what we are thinking, what we want them to do, think and feel, it creates a passive receiving and defensive reacting response. I needed to create buy in. I changed course and met with each administrative assistant to find out what her interests, goals and dreams were. The meetings were very interesting, engaging, and insightful. I learned more about each person on the team than I could have ever learned in a group meeting. We talked about their strengths and areas where they wanted to grow. We talked about the strengths of the team and possible ways we could help our organization be successful. I opened up and became vulnerable. I shared my goals and dreams with them as well. Together we brainstormed what our team goals could become. As the conversation moved from guarded to engaged, we talked about many possibilities and inspired one another to more possibilities.

Just as you need to know the style and interests of your manager, you also need to know the style and interests of those on your team. Know what lights them up and let them know you notice it. "You totally light up when you talk about that!" This type of interaction allows your team to see you care about them as individuals. I've learned the best way to lead a team is to develop relationships with the team members and find out what they want to achieve, as well as their interests, goals and dreams.

Another key lesson for me was to realize not everyone was like me. It may sound obvious or silly, but how often do we make decisions for a team based on how it would make us feel, or what we would like to happen? I'm wired with a goal-oriented and high achiever mindset. There are times I grow weary or exhausted and step away from this bent. However, I always go back; it's just how I'm wired. I've learned not everyone is this way. When I lead a team and focus only on the goal-oriented, high achiever mindset, I'm losing some of the team members because I'm not treating them as individuals or playing to their unique interests and strengths.

> "The task of leadership is not to put
> greatness into people, but to elicit it,
> for the greatness is there already."
>
> **–JOHN BUCHAN**

I've had the opportunity to lead several of my administrative teams through a Personality Style workshop and assessment. The information we learned together and about one another was highly valuable to the team. We all walked away knowing one another's strengths and preferred styles of communication. This information served us well in knowing how to interact with one another as well as knowing how to utilize our strengths and our diversity in our team goals and activities.

"What counts in life is not the mere fact that we have lived. It is what difference we have made to the lives of others that will determine the significance of the life we lead."

**–NELSON MANDELA**

Administrative assistants demonstrate leadership when they know the strengths of the individuals on their teams and inspire their teams to utilize their strengths.

### ARTICULATE THE VISION

I've learned through trial and error, the best way a leader can lead a team through establishing a vision is to get to know the team members. Draft a vision based on the team's strengths, interests and abilities. Then, share the "draft" vision with the team and create a setting where the team knows this is a place to start and it's up to the team to take this "draft vision" and openly and candidly morph it into the team's vision. I can't stress enough how important it is for the vision to be the team's vision. If you mandate the vision, it will not be followed or owned by the team, especially if you don't have direct authority over the team you are attempting to lead. You, as the leader, may experience a short period where the team members seem like they are on board. They may nod their heads in the meeting in what looks like an agreement; however, outside of the meeting, they won't express the same sentiment. I've learned, all too painfully, if the vision is mandated, the vision will not be followed long-term or owned by the team.

There are two steps to uniting a team. The first step is developing a team purpose. There is nothing that bonds a team together more than having a common purpose. It unites the team. A united purpose enables the team to act and communicates the importance of each team member. A common purpose is what turns "me" into "we."

The second step is communicating the team vision. You need to be able to articulate the vision clearly enough that the team members know where they are going and why. They need to know who is going to do what and how. With a clear vision, the team will be empowered to use their strengths to reach the desired goal. When a leader paints the picture clearly enough, the team will see why the vision is important. An effective leader doesn't separate himself from the group he leads; instead he acts as the glue that holds the team together.

> Administrative assistants demonstrate influence by facilitating the creation of a team vision and empowering their team to get involved.

## ART OF INFLUENCE

The best definition I've heard for influence is "leadership." If you are going to get anywhere in your career, you need to have influence. It is needed:

1. To get something you want.

2. To get something your executive wants or needs.

3. To reach a desired or expected outcome.

Many of us don't think we're influential. However, all of us have influence to some degree. Most administrative assistants interact with a wide variety of people. Think about your circle of influence.

1. Who do you ask to help convince your manager about something?

2. Who do you bounce ideas off of?

3. Who bounces ideas off of you?

4. Who do your vendors try to influence?

5. When you're arranging meetings with clients, what do you say to try to get on their calendars?

6. Who asks you for information?

7. Who asks to get on your manager's calendar?

8. Who needs your help?

9. Who asks you to help convince the manager about something?

When you consider the answers to these questions, you begin to realize how many people you influence on a routine basis. Without influence, you can't get the results you need. As you begin to see your own circle of influence and persuasion, you realize you are in a role to influence others and others try to influence you. Others know how crucial you are to your organization and how much power you have.

I often hear administrative assistants say the most difficult aspect of leadership is leading without authority. As administrative assistants, we may not have authority; however, the opportunity to influence is at our fingertips. We need to embrace the power of influence and have enough courage and confidence to develop and use our ability to influence others. The best place to begin using your power of influence is within your "circle of influence and persuasion" meaning those that you interact with the most and who need something from you.

Interestingly, we influence those around us without even thinking about it. It happens at a subconscious level. For example, think about the last time you went to a movie and absolutely loved it. More than likely, you came back to work the next day and told your circle of co-workers all about the movie, right? You elaborately highlighted the best parts, utilized your best acting skills and re-enacted some of the best scenes. You got their attention and did your best to "influence" them to see the movie. What is so different about this example than a work example? When you believe in your ideas and know you can contribute to reach the best possible outcome, you need to speak up and share your truth. Just as when you are sharing a great movie with friends and colleagues, you need to embrace some creativity to develop intrigue to get others to listen to your point of view and solution to a particular challenge. The more you practice your ability to influence, the easier it will become to utilize. It can actually be a lot of fun.

One of the most common ways administrative assistants influence others is through our expertise. You demonstrate leadership and influence, when you share your expertise. You influence others leveraging your reputation and earning respect by becoming known as the "go to person."

# Administrative assistants are influential when they rise up to the call of leadership.

## WORDS MATTER

You can influence people positively or negatively by the words you speak. Words have energy. Choose positive and inspirational words. Choose to focus on and talk about what is working. Everyone is already aware of what isn't working and what is wrong. The more we talk about what's not working, the bigger the situation becomes. We are giving the problem energy to grow and become worse than it is. You can influence others in a positive way by using uplifting and encouraging words and get ahead.

Administrative assistants have a lot of inside information others don't have. We can choose to gossip and talk negatively about staff members or we can choose to tell others positive news stories. Using judgment and reason, we need to share our knowledge freely with others. Be known as the person who helps others solve problems and get ahead.

It's also important to choose how we refer to each other and to our manager. It is my goal that we, as administrative assistants, stop saying, "I'm 'just' an admin." Equally important is to stop referring to the administrative staff you work with as "the girls in the office." I've never heard a man say, "The guys in the office." This vocabulary is old school and puts us in a less than positive light. It's also important to refer to your boss as your executive or manager. When we use the term "boss," it doesn't sound as professional nor does it paint a picture of a powerful partnership.

Consider your words carefully. They have tremendous power and people will judge you based on the words you use.

> ## Administrative assistants demonstrate leadership by choosing their words carefully.

## CHARISMA

One of the most powerful methods of leadership and influence is charisma. It may feel elusive and difficult to develop, but it will be well worth the effort. Charisma is powerful. Charisma is defined as having a personal quality that gives an individual influence or authority over people.

If you believe you are not naturally charismatic, here are some simple things you can do to increase your charisma:

1. Smile! It makes you approachable and puts others at ease.

2. Be genuinely interested in others.

3. Call the person you are talking to by name.

4. Be a good listener.

5. Be externally focused.

6. Care about every person in the group.

7. Walk with certainty.

8. Exude self-confidence.

9. Make other people feel important.

My husband is one of the most charismatic people I know. Yet, years ago, he was incredibly shy and stuttered. When he was in high school, he forced himself to change by becoming a waiter which required him to talk to people. He was a life learner and observed others. He watched how his friend's parents interacted. He learned from those he observed and, over time, he became a great communicator. At his core, he truly loves people and is interested in others. When he smiles, he lights up the room and attracts others. He is outwardly focused and others know he cares about them as he intently listens to the conversation. You can do this, too! All it takes is focused effort, practice, time and genuinely caring about others.

# Administrative assistants demonstrate leadership when they are externally focused.

## COLLABORATION VERSUS COMPETITION

To succeed in today's world, you must collaborate. Years ago, collaboration wasn't as easy; we didn't have email and videoconferencing tools like we have today. We have many tools at our fingertips which make connection and collaboration easy. Wikipedia describes collaboration as "working with each other to do a task and to achieve shared goals." When we collaborate, we increase the success for all involved, including our company. Collaboration is a powerful way to accomplish what no single person can do on her own. When we don't collaborate, our thoughts and ideas are limited. You can have the best idea but without a team with whom you can collaborate, you can't get your idea off the ground.

When you join forces with others, many more ideas are created and resources to implement ideas are increased.

"As you navigate through the rest of your life,
be open to collaboration.

Other people and other people's ideas
are often better than your own.

Find a group of people, who challenge and inspire
you, spend a lot of time with them,
and it will change your life."

**–AMY POEHLER**

When we work in a mode of competition, we have a tendency to think of knowledge as power and do our best to hold onto all our power. We don't want anyone to have more information or more knowledge than we have. We are not inspired or motivated to share our knowledge, we are fearful of someone outplaying us and losing, so we hide and protect what we have so we don't lose our competitive edge

I'm a highly competitive person; however, I've learned competition in the workplace isn't as productive as collaboration. A competitive spirit often means I win, you lose. I love competition especially when I'm playing a sport, a board game, or cards…just ask my family and they will tell you!

The Academy of Management Journal featured a story about a study done by Bianca Beersma, John Hollenbeck, Stephen Humphrey, Henry Moon, Donald Conlon and Daniel LIgen proving if you want the job done fast, competition is the way to go. If you want the job done well, you're better off with cooperation and collaboration. The study also proved keeping up in a competitive society increases stress, elevates blood pressure, and leads to life-shortening effects.

A confident and experienced leader knows he doesn't have all the answers. When he admits this to the team, the team knows he has a spirit of collaboration. When the leader gets out of the way of his team, the team members are empowered to utilize their strengths and talents to their greatest capacity. When the leader tells the team, no one succeeds alone, that individual success is attached to the team's success; the team knows collaboration is key.

# Administrative assistants demonstrate leadership and influence through collaborating with others to help others succeed.

Administrative assistants are leaders! Administrative assistants interact with many people and touch many lives. When administrative assistants aren't around, we definitely leave a gap in our work groups and organizations. Our behaviors and our interactions shape those who are around us. Whether we intend to or not, our presence affects others. We all choose what actions we take and how we communicate.

"There is a choice you
have to make in everything you do.

So keep in mind that in the end,
the choice you make, makes you."

**–JOHN WOODEN**

Choose your words carefully, share appropriate information freely, and uplift those with whom you interact to encourage them to move past their comfort zones. When you give of yourself to help others succeed, the success will come back to you tenfold. You will know you have made a difference in someone's life…what more can we expect from a leader?

"If your actions inspire others to dream more,
learn more, do more and become more,
you are a leader."

**–JOHN QUINCY ADAMS**

# Yes, I've Been Fired!

"I didn't see it then, but it turned out that getting fired from Apple was the best thing that could have ever happened to me."

**–STEVE JOBS**

## CHAPTER**EIGHT**

# Yes, I've Been Fired!

I was the office manager for a small company. I thought things were going well as I had been given more responsibility than originally hired to handle and I was contributing at a higher level than expected. Even though this experience happened years ago, I can clearly remember the emotions I felt as my manager called me into her office to meet with her partner and herself.

## I've learned you can keep going, long after you think you can't.

I was completely shocked when they told me they were letting me go because they didn't think I wanted to work! I had no idea this was coming. I hadn't received any warning. No one had told me they were unhappy with my performance. I had a great attendance record and thought I was getting along well with the team.

My mind was screaming, "What! I don't want to work? Are you kidding me?" I'm sure my mouth must have dropped wide open. I don't remember how I responded. All I can remember is I was expecting my second child and my husband was on disability due to a work related back injury. Not only did I want to work, I had no choice but to work. I was the only one in my family able to work at the time and needed the job for the income and the insurance benefits. How was this happening? Why was this happening?

I left the office in sheer disbelief. My mind was racing with questions. What was I going to do? What was going to happen? I called my husband to tell him the bad news and let him know I was going straight to Manpower (a temporary job agency) and the Unemployment Office before coming home. He was as shocked as I was and provided me some much needed words of encouragement.

Manpower put me to work right away and sent me on several temporary assignments. I was grateful and relieved to have work so I could care for my family. One day, I came home and while going through the mail, I saw an envelope from the unemployment office. To my surprise, it wasn't an unemployment check, it was a letter informing me my former employer was fighting my unemployment claim and an arbitration hearing had been scheduled. Once again, I couldn't believe it! Why was my former manager suddenly my worst enemy?

By the time the hearing occurred, I was several months pregnant. I still had no idea why my former manager felt I didn't want to work, fired me, and denied my unemployment claim. I thought there had to be something more to the decision than what they had shared with me. However, I had no insight into what the reason could be.

I remember looking across the conference table at my former managers wondering what had happened. I desperately wanted to end the formality of the hearing and just ask them what had happened to make them think I didn't want to work. I was young and had no idea what to do, other than to tell the truth, which is exactly what I did. After an hour or so, the arbitrator ruled in my favor as my former managers had no proof to back their claim stating I didn't want to work and I had proof I was working, doing all that was requested, and receiving positive feedback.

I was relieved to have the outcome in my favor, but I was still confused about why they chose to fire me and even more puzzling was the fact that they went so far as to fight the unemployment claim. This experience happened a long time ago. Since that time, I've learned things happen at work which we may never understand or know the reasoning behind the decisions. We likely want closure to understand the decisions, and often the closure and information we are seeking is not revealed to us. The only thing we can do is let go of the past, learn the most we can from it, and focus on the future so we can move forward.

In my case, I learned six months or so after the arbitration had passed that my former employers had gone out of business and closed their doors due to financial pressures. Finally, a possible reason for firing me and fighting the unemployment insurance claim surfaced.

Within a few months, I landed a temporary position through Manpower that later turned into a permanent position. It was a great company, great staff, and a great manager. I enjoyed working with them, had the opportunity to increase my skill set by working with two Boards of Directors, and was thriving in my position. I worked for this company for seven years and only left because I had my third child and wanted to take a year off to be with my children. In many ways being fired propelled me forward.

# Destiny is not where you are now, but where you are going.

# Your present situation is not your final destination.

The story gets better. Years went by and my children were grown. I was working for a new company. I was at work one day, doing my normal routine, when I received an internal email from that former manager who fired me! I was completely shocked to find out she was now working at the same company where I was working! Imagine the odds of that happening! Her email started out with a caring sentiment, asking about my children, how old they were, how many children I had, how everyone was doing and then moved on to ask me for a favor. A favor! Are you kidding me? She wanted to know if I could help her son obtain an internship.

You can imagine my shock and surprise when I heard from her. I thought, "After everything you did to me and my family and now you want me to help you and your family!" A huge part of me wanted to respond in the meanest, most nasty way I could imagine so I could get my revenge. I considered many options. I thought about deleting her email and acting as if I never received it. I considered ignoring the email and never responding. That would show her! I gave it a lot of thought. I read and re-read the email.

Thankfully, I waited a day or so before responding. (There's a lesson or two here.)

Instead of getting even, taking full advantage of the situation, and having the opportunity to experience my sweet revenge, I realized when it came down to it, there was really only one thing I could do. Take the high road. I didn't want to take the high road, but I knew nothing else really made sense in the long run.

What does it mean to take the high road? It's simple: Don't keep score. Forgive others quickly. Learn to serve. Don't get even. Live a life that will serve you and others well.

The high road isn't easy, and not many people choose to take this road. It's definitely a road less traveled because it requires people to think and do things that are not natural or common. In my case, it really wasn't the action I wanted to take, yet I am grateful I made the right decision.

I've made my share of mistakes, plenty of them, and I've had the experience of someone forgiving me. When you hear someone say, "Don't worry about it." "We don't need to talk about this again." "You are forgiven" – and you know in your heart you're totally forgiven, you'll never forget it. It's an act of grace that will melt your heart with gratefulness and humility. A moment of grace can change your life forever.

I am grateful I've had people in my life demonstrate what it means to take the high road and who forgave me for my mistakes. The strength and compassion shown to me in my most vulnerable moments is what provided me the strength to demonstrate strength, compassion, and grace to another later in my journey.

# When something bad happens you have three choices.

# You can either let it define you, let it destroy you, or you can let it strengthen you.

Whenever you are in the position of strength and/or being right and the person you are facing is in a position of weakness and/ or clearly wrong, you win by taking the high road! Taking the high road becomes sweeter than any revenge you could imagine. Knowing you did the right thing when you had the opportunity to take full advantage of someone who had wronged you, increases your inner strength and character.

Choosing to take the high road isn't easy and doesn't come naturally, but it's the strongest position to take on the journey through life. When you consider how everything we do and say comes back to us, there really is no other choice but to take the high road.

When I look back on the day I was fired compared to where I am now, both in my career and as a person, being fired was the best thing that could have happened to me. It certainly wasn't easy at the time. I was crushed, devastated, and completely confused. However, I overcame the obstacle, found an even better position and continued to grow. I doubt all of this would have occurred if I would have remained in that small office.

> # Be grateful for all the obstacles in your life.
>
> # They have strengthened you as you continued with your journey.

I am grateful I had a positive mental attitude and could rise up from being knocked down. I know it was all those years of reading books by Norman Vincent Peale and John Maxwell that helped me believe in myself and have the confidence to find another position as well as to stand up to a former manager in an arbitration hearing.

There are many times in life when you will need to choose to take the high road. One of those times is when you are being attacked or criticized. I've learned if you're going to do anything great in life, if you're going to be a great administrative assistant, a great parent, or a great leader, you need to understand not everyone is going to cheer you on. I'd love to tell you that your family, friends and co-workers will celebrate you, but often that is not the case. Some people simply can't handle your success. As you grow and increase, somebody will get jealous. Somebody will start finding fault. Don't be surprised if a relative tries to belittle you or a co-worker tries to discredit you. Greatness in the midst of criticism begins with forgiveness. Don't hold a grudge against people who are trying to hold you down.

Have you ever noticed there isn't a lid on a crab pot? The reason is if one of the crabs tries to crawl out, one of the other crabs will pull him back down. All of the crabs stay in the crab pot together making sure no one rises to the top. Sometimes life feels like you are a crab in a crab pot, filled with lots of other crabs. Every time you crawl up towards the top, one of the crabs pulls you back down. This really isn't about you. It's about the insecurities of others and how your success and hard work causes others to feel uncomfortable. The crabs would be so much happier if you would just stay in the bottom of the crab pot where you could commiserate in your misery together.

Instead of worrying about settling the score or trying to make everyone like you, know you are making a difference by performing at a high level. Your actions may make some people feel uncomfortable. They can also serve as a source of inspiration and motivate others to increase their level of performance.

People will talk about you whether you are a high performer or a low performer. Some people love to talk and gossip about one another. No matter what others are saying, there is no need to change your actions to be liked or approved of by the masses.

Instead, just keep taking the high road, do the right thing, treat others with grace, don't keep score, forgive others quickly, and do the very best job you can do. I'll see you on the high road!

"Believe in yourself and all that you are.

Know that there is something inside you that is greater than any obstacle."

**—CHRISTIAN LARSON**

# A Mentor Can Make All the Difference

"There is no exercise better for the heart
than reaching down and lifting people up."

CHAPTER**NINE**

# A Mentor Can Make All the Difference

Each of us was designed for greatness. To be our best, we need to become our best unique self. We don't need to become a "mini-me" of another great person. Sure, it's natural to emulate someone we admire, but we need to stay true to who we are. When we strive to become like someone else, we will always be small – a mini version of someone else. When we play to our strengths, we can become more than we dreamed of...more than we imagined.

## THE POWER OF MENTORING

Since I was a little girl, I had the desire to connect with others and encourage them to become all they could be. Perhaps this is why I became an executive assistant and chose to support executives. In this position, I play a key role in the success of the executives I support. I provide feedback, counsel, insight, information and encouragement. I ask strategic questions to steer them in the right direction. The support I provide enables them to use their strengths and resources to achieve more than they could achieve alone – which is exactly what a mentor can do for you.

We all need a mentor to teach us and lift us up from where we are and help us get to where we want to be.

I've sought out a variety of mentors over the years. My first mentors were my grandparents, parents and teachers. My grandparents taught me what it means to love someone unconditionally. My grandmother often said, "There are no bad people, some people just choose to behave badly for a really long time."

My parents taught me the importance of hard work, resourcefulness, and the value of a family. My father and his father were in the road construction business, as were many of my uncles and cousins. They were proud to be in the "union" and work hard to provide a good life for their families. My dad made it a rule to only take jobs where he could drive to the work location and home in the same day in order to be with his family. When summer came, he often took jobs in the mountains building logging roads where he could take the whole family with him. It was a great environment for our family to live in the mountains all summer long.

We were living deep in the woods where there wasn't a town or modern conveniences for miles around. We only had each other and, most of the time, we got along really well. One of the most exciting parts of our day was running up to the log road to signal the log truck drivers to blow their horns for us.

In this environment, I quickly learned what it meant to be resourceful. My dad used his creativity and resourcefulness to turn tree logs into furniture; we had a long log with three scoops in it for our sofa and two smaller stumps carved out just right for my mom and dad's chairs complete with foot rests. We sat in these around the camp fire for cooking and storytelling each evening.

One of the most resourceful moments was when my two sisters and I were very young and my dad had a job opportunity in Alaska. Dad purchased a used milk truck, painted it, put in a sink, fridge, countertops and a port-a-potty. He stacked three metal bunk beds one on top of the other and bolted them to the floor. My mom did her best to make our new "motor home" into a home for us for the long drive from Washington State to Alaska. Mom was definitely more patient than I could fully appreciate at the time. Her chair was a folding lawn chair which would often be off balance and fall over! We took a hamster, a mouse and a gerbil as well as our dog with us, all packed into our make shift motor home. I'm sure we looked like Jed Clampett and the Beverly Hillbillies! What great memories!

At the time, I thought everything was great and this was another great adventure. However, looking back, we came from some pretty humble beginnings.

I've had some incredible teachers who served as mentors by believing in me and making me feel special by doing what was needed to teach me what I needed to learn. I can remember a grade school teacher who realized I didn't know how to tell time even though I was sporting a large white leather watch. She was kind enough to keep my secret quiet and help me after school.

While I was in high school, I was in DECA, an international association of high school and college students and teachers of marketing, management and entrepreneurship in business. I am very thankful for this opportunity as I learned many valuable lessons in those two years. I learned about dressing for interviews and interviewing skills as well as business etiquette and presentation skills. The most important lesson was about reputation. Through DECA, I received my first job as a secretary, working part time after school for a small furniture company. This was long before computers, or even the modern "Selectric" typewriter. I typed on a manual typewriter, used carbon paper in triplicate, had colored white-out, and the copy paper was wet when it came out of the machine! For those of you who haven't experienced this past technology, trust me, it was a whole different world.

I had been working for this company for a few months when one day my DECA teacher asked to meet with me after class.

He asked, "How is your job going?" "It's going great." I responded

We continued talking for a few minutes. I don't remember everything he said. I only remember he was kind and caring. I remember, like it was yesterday, him showing me an example of my work and asking, "Is this your work?"

I glanced at the first letter and it was filled with mistakes and white out. I quickly turned to the next letter hoping it was better, but to my embarrassment it, too, was messy and unprofessional. I wanted to respond with, "No, this isn't my work." The problem was...it was my work! I was humiliated and hesitantly responded, "Yes, this is my work."

He then asked me the most impressionable question I've ever been asked:

"Is this what you want your reputation to be?"

My heart sank! I uttered a tearful response, *"I don't want to be known for sloppy work. I don't want to be considered a failure or a poor performer!"*

I don't remember anything else my teacher said. All I felt then and know now was he believed in me, he was kind, he didn't berate me, and he didn't make me feel small. Instead, he wanted to help me. He showed he cared about me enough to talk my employer into letting me keep my job and prove I could do better and become a strong performer. My employer agreed and I had the opportunity to prove my abilities.

That moment of mentoring was life changing.

As I was writing this chapter, I heard on the news that Maya Angelo had passed away. She has been a mentor from afar for me for years. Whenever I read something she's written, or watched her speak, I found myself smiling on the outside and the inside. She exuded so much wisdom and strength. I also loved her humbleness and compassion as well as her zest for life. I love so many Maya Angelo quotes. Some of my favorites are: "You should make it to 80 if you can, the 80's are hot!" "Moderation in all things, even moderation in moderation!" and "The only thing that heals is love." I've watched and recorded several of her interviews and am always delighted to listen to her stories. I love the way she weaves her messages of strength, encouragement, overcoming challenges, and victory all while being humble, yet confident. I am grateful she made the decision to "rise" and overcome her challenges so she could make a powerful impression on all of us and lift us to new places that we may not have found on our own. She has been a tremendous mentor and her teachings will continue even though she has passed.

> "If you get, give. If you learn, teach."
> **—MAYA ANGELOU**

Another mentor from afar is John Maxwell. I've learned a great deal from him about the power of a positive mental attitude and what it means to be a leader. One of the lessons which impacted me the most is "Swing the bat!" John tells a story about his nephew, Eric, in his first little league game. Eric's parents weren't able to attend, so John and his wife, Margaret, attended to support

Eric. John reminds us how vicious parents can behave at little league games and how serious the coaches can be. In John's view, little league is pretty hilarious and should be fun. The game began and the coach started yelling at Eric. John didn't appreciate the coach's negative approach, so John took his nephew to the side and told him, "Eric, baseball is a very simple game. All you have to do is swing the bat every time the pitcher throws the ball. Don't worry about anything else, just swing the bat." Eric said, "I can do that." Eric got up to the plate and even though he missed the first ball, the second ball and the third ball and struck out, John stood up and applauded and yelled, "Great job Eric! Way to swing the bat!" The coach looked at John like he was crazy.

John's point is if you swing the bat, you increase the odds of connecting and of the ball hitting the bat. When Eric got up the next time to bat, he swung the bat and connected with the ball. It didn't go far, but it was fair. John got up out of his seat and ran down on the field to run with his nephew around the bases. Eric made it all the way around the bases and slid into home base!

When they got home, they did a reenactment for Eric's parents in their living room. The story was filled with excitement and enthusiasm. Every time John and Eric get together, they tell this story. Years later, Eric called John to let him know what he learned from him and the importance of swinging the bat and confessed that he remembers this lesson and applies it to his life. He also wanted to let John know he was going to college on a baseball scholarship!

# Never discount the power of mentoring!

Another mentoring moment for me was attending conferences. I've heard many speakers throughout my career and learned a great deal from what they shared. I was also moved by their inspirational stories and passion. I took massive notes and wanted to be more and do more in my life.

One of my most impactful conference experiences was when I heard Judi Moreo speak at an Administrative Professionals Conference. Judi is an author and an international speaker and is the founder and owner of Turning Point International. Her wisdom and inspiration lets her audience members know she believes in you. Her confidence and passion radiate out of her and make you feel stronger. I wanted to learn and take in all she had to share.

From the very beginning, I felt a connection with Judi. I resonated with her and her topics. The spark I had as a young child about becoming a writer was rekindled. I couldn't ignore the feelings stirring inside of me. The dream that was first planted in me to be a writer was bursting alive. As I listened to Judi and thought of all the past speakers I had heard, I realized my favorite moments had always been encouraging and inspiring others. My dream became crystal clear - I wanted to be a writer and a speaker! It was daunting for me to voice my dream to others. I wanted it so badly and didn't want anyone to laugh or criticize me. I didn't have the confidence I needed to be a writer and a speaker. However, I couldn't deny the voice inside of me telling me this was my purpose and exactly what I was supposed to do. I knew I needed someone to help me get to where I wanted to go and I couldn't get there alone. At times, I wasn't even sure where "there" was; I just knew I wanted more and had more in me to give.

So I began.

I began by having enough courage to approach Judi. I introduced myself to her and thanked her for her class. It was a little intimidating and I must admit I was nervous to make the first move.

I was pleasantly surprised to find her approachable and kind. She offered me an opportunity to sign up for her newsletter, and asked me to follow up with her to let her know what I thought. And I did! I did exactly what she asked. How many times does someone extend an opportunity to us and we don't allow the door to open? Take the risk! Don't let your fear paralyze you and close the door on an opportunity that is right before you.

I became a subscriber to Judi's newsletter and read her books. Judi had more knowledge than I had. She had experienced more success than I had and, therefore, was in the perfect position to help me grow. She became my mentor from afar, probably without even knowing it at first.

Then as our relationship began to grow, I emailed Judi for advice now and then. I remember the day when I answered the phone and it was Judi! She was calling me! She knew I had been facing a difficult meeting and wanted to know how things went. It was at that moment I knew she was a true mentor to me. Over the years, our relationship has continued to develop and has grown into one that is mutually beneficial. I was honored when she asked me to do some writing for her and when she used a few of my quotes and articles. She made me feel brilliant and talented. One day, she asked me to be a contributing author for her book, *Life Choices - Putting the Pieces Together.* I'd always wanted to be an author and here was an opportunity to realize that dream. We talked about what she needed from me in order for me to be approved as a contributing author and I met the challenge. I thought about what to write and decided on mentoring. I submitted my chapter, "The Mentoring Mirror: Seeing Yourself Through the Eyes of a Mentor." My chapter was approved and printed in the *Life Choices – Putting the Pieces Together* book! I was so excited to have my first part in a book. When the box of books arrived, I couldn't wait to rip open the box and see, touch and smell the book. I quickly turned to my chapter to make sure it was real and see my picture on the back cover. It was real! I had accomplished a small piece of my dream and I owe much of my success of becoming a writer to Judi.

"You are more than enough."
**–JUDI MOREO**

In addition, I began working with a group of individuals focused on leadership and staff development who also became my mentors. Together, we created programs to empower and teach others. We focused on developing them into better managers, leaders, and, ultimately, better people. I thrived in this position and soaked up all the knowledge I could. I read everything available to me and observed the trainers and participants. I learned what resonated well with the participants and what didn't. I learned different approaches and methods. My role was diverse: I worked behind the scenes, helped develop training materials, participated as a student in the classroom, and provided training to our participants.

One day, my manager asked me to become a certified trainer and introduced me to a certification program. I was excited and scared at the same time. Knowing she believed in me enough to invest in me and increase my training and speaking abilities meant a great deal to me. I stepped out of my comfort zone and agreed to enroll in the certification program.

The program was intense and required each participant to speak in front of the class while being recorded via video camera. There were about ten people in the program and we were all nervous. We had an afternoon and evening to prepare topics and create our presentations. I researched my topic and rehearsed in my hotel room until I was tired of hearing myself talk. When I woke up in the morning, I started rehearsing again and praying!

Each of us was called one-by-one for our turn to give our presentations. When my name was called, my heart skipped a beat. I told myself, "This is all part of the process and I am here to learn." I took the speakers position and to my surprise, everything I had rehearsed came out exactly as planned. I didn't forget, I didn't stutter, and I didn't make a fool of myself.

Another aspect of the class was giving and receiving feedback. The instructor and the students all provided feedback to each speaker. Sure, I had plenty to improve upon but my first presentation wasn't bad. In fact, it went pretty well. We helped each other as we knew we were all there to learn and improve our skill sets. As the days went by, speaking and giving and receiving feedback got easier.

The process of becoming a certified trainer was at times nerve-racking, but the majority of it was energizing. I am so grateful my manager and co-workers believed enough in me to invest in my talents and abilities. Becoming certified and providing training to managers was a huge opportunity and a growing experience. It forced me to stretch out of my comfort zone and risk failing while learning a new skill. Multiply being new at training and speaking by being an admin and providing training to managers - people who were in a higher position than me and had more education than me and you have a perfect environment for a disaster. However, that isn't what happened. It wasn't always easy and, at times, I was questioned about my education and background. I was able to overcome the questions posed to me and pull off the training as planned. Inside, I may have been shaking, but I wasn't about to crumble. I took a deep breath and met the challenge.

I am very thankful for becoming certified and for the opportunity to provide training for the first time. It boosted my confidence and reassured me that I had enough talent to make a reality of my dream of becoming a speaker, trainer, and writer.

> "You never know when one kind act or one word of encouragement can change a life forever."
> **–ZIG ZIGLAR**

## THANKING A MENTOR

One day, one of my mentors at work retired. She had played a key role in helping identify the position with the leadership and staff development team for me. If it wasn't for her involvement, it is highly unlikely I would have known about the opportunity or would have applied. The position was perfectly aligned with my ability, interests, and desires. A memory book was created for her retirement celebration and this is what I wrote:

> *"I remember meeting you during an interview for a new position...During the interview you did something unique...you listened! You took the time to really assess who I was, what my strengths and interests were, and where I would be most successful.*
>
> *Because you took the time to listen, you later encouraged me to apply for a position...Even though I didn't know much about this group, I trusted you and applied for the position. Not only did I land the position, but it was one of the best experiences in my career. I had the blessing of working with a group of people who were all truly passionate about their positions and wanted to make a difference for others. I received a priceless amount of information and a wealth of knowledge from this position. I have no doubt the knowledge I obtained from this experience has directly attributed to who and where I am today.*

*Know that you are the type of person everyone needs in her career...someone who cares and is interested in her as an individual and shows her the "door of opportunity" where her skill set and strengths can be best utilized.*

*Thank you for all you have done for me – your support has been outstanding and appreciated!*

*You will be greatly missed!"*

## IDENTIFYING A MENTOR

Do you have a mentor? If not, where do you go for counsel and advice? Have you identified someone you want to be your mentor? Have you asked someone to be your mentor?

When you are looking for a mentor, find someone who has more knowledge and experience than you. Find someone who is where you want to be. Look for a mentor who has similar values to yours. Once you identify your mentor, there are a few things you need to do and understand:

1. The responsibility to develop the relationship is yours.

2. Be respectful of your mentor's time.

3. Let your mentor know why you want to be mentored by him or her.

4. Communicate what you want to learn.

5. Follow through on the advice and counsel you receive.

## BE A MENTOR

When you've gone through struggles in your life, your ability to detect struggles in others' lives is heightened. You can give someone the gift of a lesson you've learned so they won't have to learn that lesson firsthand. You can spare someone a painful experience. The same is true for success. When you've experienced success, you can help someone else succeed. You can share your story, your experiences, and show someone else how to navigate a path you've already traveled.

# Share your knowledge, there's enough room in this world for all of us to succeed.

I've had wonderful mentors in my life and because of the mentoring I've received, I became a more effective mentor to others. As I grew in my administrative and training career, and as I learned through experiences and reading, my ability to mentor others also grew.

I've also found my experience of supporting executives and providing training created the perfect foundation to successfully mentor others. I used strategic questioning to point them toward a new pathway. I reminded them of their goals and priorities and discussed what actions they could take to help them get where they wanted to go. I was a trusted confidant. I expressed my confidence in their abilities and challenged them to step out of their comfort zones. All of these things inspired them to grow and believe in themselves more than they had previously.

As a mentor, I also looked for opportunities to shine for those I was mentoring. As I was blessed with opportunities for growth and development, I found ways to include others. One of my former co-workers has often said she rode on my coattails for all they were worth and took in all that was offered. According to her, the dream of speaking at a national conference wouldn't have been realized without my involvement and mentoring.

## DEVELOPING A MENTORING PROGRAM

I had an amazing opportunity of working with a group of talented executive assistants. Together, we created and implemented a mentoring program for the administrative assistants in our organization. This was a rich and rewarding experience.

Some of my mentoring relationships have been a part of a formal mentoring program, some have been more casual and about a single process or topic. Other times, mentoring is being a role model or coaching someone to a new level. Mentoring is helping others with what they need in order to move forward.

To mentor effectively, follow these steps:

1. Let others know you believe in them.

2. Share your knowledge and experience.

3. Find opportunities for others to shine.

4. Help others step out of their comfort zones.

5. Lift others up through their challenges.

6. Be a role model.

7. Be vulnerable, allow others to see the real you.

8. Keep confidences.

## MENTORING STORY

One of my favorite mentoring experiences is about someone who is like many of us. She's someone to whom most of us can relate…someone filled with potential bursting at the seams, yet she doesn't quite see her potential and talent. She doesn't have the confidence in herself to believe she really can do all the things she wants to do. It's hard for her to verbalize her dreams. She wants to be a leader, and influence others, but she is doubtful in her abilities. She's afraid of being mocked or ridiculed for her dreams.

We all have so much to offer the world, if only we could see our own greatness instead of holding ourselves back from the possibilities of success. We're afraid of standing out too much. We have talent and potential within us. The challenge most of us face is accepting and acknowledging our greatness. This typically is because we're afraid. And so it was with her. She was afraid she would fail or be criticized. How many times have you felt this way?

I told her, "We're all afraid and we all doubt ourselves. None of us wants to fail. The only thing that builds confidence is action. We need to take the first step forward even when we're afraid, even when we might fail, be wrong or are judged. A leader doesn't have to have all the answers. In fact, the more vulnerable we are as leaders, the more approachable and real we will be to those we are leading. Leaders need to take responsibility for their actions and press on to meet the desired outcome. Leaders need to care about those they are leading and be able to make tough decisions. Leaders need to do what needs to be done even when they are tired and when the task is difficult. Leaders need to do what is best, even when it's painful. Leaders must deliver the right messages, not just the message someone wants to hear. The best part of saying yes to leadership is that we learn. We learn from our mistakes and from our successes, and with that knowledge and experience we become more confident and more skilled. There is no short cut; you just have to be willing to say yes to the opportunities that come your way."

Once she understood I had similar feelings, her confidence increased. She understood I had fears and doubts just as she did but I chose to take action any way. She realized taking action was exactly what she needed to do as well. She also learned we had much more in common than she had realized. She had put me on a pedestal because I was in a higher position than she was. She now saw the real me and knew I was there to help her and desired the best for her.

## CALL TO ACTION!

I challenge you to look in the mirror – who do you see? Can you see yourself as a mentor sees you? A mentor sees potential and possibilities inside you. A mentor sees you making a difference by living your dream and inspiring others to greatness because of your actions. Who are you mentoring? For whom are you a role model? Who will you inspire because of your actions? Will you be bold enough to see yourself as a mentor sees you? You have the answers to your mentoring challenge.

> Never underestimate the power of influencing another through mentoring, it can be life changing!

# Keeping the Passion, Goals, and Dreams Alive

"Make It Happen!"

CHAPTER**TEN**

# Keeping the Passion, Goals, and Dreams Alive

When I was in grade school and was asked, "What do you want to be when you grow up?" My answer was, "A movie star!" Not an actress…a movie star! It must have been all those old glamorous movies with Ginger Rogers and Fred Astaire or Doris Day and Rock Hudson that I watched while growing up. My current dream of being a speaker and a writer isn't that far away from my childhood dream. After all, there's still a stage (and often a camera) involved, however, that certainly isn't the glamorous life I envisioned as a young starry eyed girl.

The reality of making your dreams happen is hard work. No one becomes a success overnight. There are years of hard work and sacrifice involved before we hear about the new rising star that has become an "overnight success."

While writing this book, I had to decline many invitations that I would have jumped at if I wasn't focused and determined to finish writing. Friends called inviting my husband and me to spend the afternoon boating on the river, going to the movies, and spending the evening on the patio enjoying great food and friends. Weekend getaways and the like were mostly met with a decline for a few months. I did take time out now and then for some down time. When I did, my dream was still beckoning to me…calling me to complete the work and realize the dream.

# Realizing your dreams means saying no to other things to make room for the thing you really want.

Saying "no" means turning down other opportunities. "No, I can't meet with you." "No, I can't come to your party." Learning to say, "No" and declining activities I really enjoyed was hard. I didn't want to miss out. However, what I wanted even more was to achieve my dream. Some people didn't understand. Some people even told me that my life was out of balance and I needed to stop being so intense…because life is short. What these people didn't understand is the reason I was so determined to complete my book is because they are right - life is short!

"No is the foundation that we can build our yes on."

**–SETH GODIN**

You know you're really living to reach your dream when you start worrying, "What if I die before I finish!" Talk about a dream giving you the motivation to live! When a dream comes from your core, from your heart, it gives you so many reasons to live. The dream becomes your purpose and you simply must keep on persevering until the dream is accomplished.

I've heard, "Your dream needs to be so big that it scares you." I embraced the idea, but I didn't really get it until I started saying "yes" to my dream more often than I said "no" to it. Deep down you probably have a dream to "be" or "do" something amazing. It may be difficult to say it out loud for fear of being criticized or judged. Often, we are the ones who judge ourselves the most. We start to dream and our minds begin to explore the possibilities. We don't get far before the voices of doubt start to speak so loudly that we can't fight it and we give into the negative thoughts. Before we know it, the glimmer of the dream we had starts to disappear. We stifle the hope, give into the negative voices, and let fear rule our lives. What if we didn't do this?

# What could we do if we believed we could not fail?

I've wanted to write a book for years. What made me finally roll up my sleeves? I could no longer NOT do it! My dream had become so strong that I could no longer deny what I wanted to do. I didn't ask anyone for permission. I didn't ask anyone if they thought I could do it. Instead, I started boldly announcing to people that I was writing a book. Doing so, built in accountability for me and it also created a support group to champion my dream. My plan was to tell so many people that I had to deliver!

Another nugget of wisdom I learned is "When your dream is big enough and important enough to you, you will pursue it even if you don't get paid." This is when you know you've found the core, the essence of your dreams. I wanted to write my book for myself, for my children, for my grandchildren and for you. I was no longer focused on writing a perfect book that everyone would love. Instead, I wanted to do it because the dream was inside of me…because I have knowledge to share. And, I wanted to prove to myself that I could do it. I wanted to touch, smell, and see my book in my hand.

Take a minute and ask yourself, "What did I want to be when I was a child?" "What would I choose to do if I knew I could not fail?" Whatever that special dream is inside of you, go for it! The years are going by and before you know it five years will have passed. What could happen in five years if you put your heart and soul into your dream?

# What are your goals and dreams?

As an administrative assistant, you may also have goals and dreams outside of your current profession. I know several administrative assistants who have furthered their educations, have become writers and speakers, and still choose to be in the administrative profession.

I am not saying being an administrative assistant isn't enough, not at all. Instead, I want you to consider what you want in every aspect of your life? If you want to be the best mom or dad on the planet, what are you doing to become the best mom or dad? If you want to become a great leader, what are you doing now to become an effective leader?

At times, someone outside of the administrative profession will say to an administrative assistant, "What's your next step? What do you want to be? I'm sure the intentions of these people are good; however, it comes across as if being an administrative assistant isn't enough. It's not often you hear a manager ask another manager this same question. If you are an administrative assistant who has chosen the administrative career, you can and should hold your head high. You are in a worthy profession and should be proud of your contribution.

You may be fortunate and have a support group to champion your dreams, and you may not be so fortunate. No matter which is the case for you, know your value and self-worth. Someone may tell you, "You are just an admin and won't be able to rise to the dreams you have for yourself." Don't buy into the limitations that others have of you. Don't shrink to allow others to feel more powerful or comfortable about themselves. Instead, stand up for yourself and show them all you have to offer this world. I know what this experience feels like. I've been there, but I'm not about to let someone else's opinion of me become my reality. Use these types of negative experiences to dig your heels in and catapult forward to prove to yourself and others all that you can do.

Whatever your dream is, it was planted in you for a purpose and only you can achieve it. You have your own unique talents, gifts, abilities, interests, passions and strengths – Use Them!

## How will your use your strengths, talents and passion to shine?

Most of us want to make a difference in this world. The best way to make a difference is to utilize your strengths in an area of passion. Your strength may be organization. You may have received countless compliments on your ability to organize materials, events and keep everything on track. You may also have a passion for curing cancer. If that is the case, you could contact the cancer association in your area and find out how to get involved with an upcoming event, or become a member of one of their committees or boards. You'd be surprised what happens when you take the initiative to reach out and volunteer your time and talents.

A volunteer activity often leads to more opportunities. The experience will further develop your skill set, give you an opportunity to shine in your area of strength, and you'll increase your network all while in the process of serving others. The serendipitous part about volunteering is you get involved to help others and what you find is the experience strengthens you, your skill set, your network, and your character along the way.

Consider the compliments you receive, what do people compliment you about most often? Whatever your strengths are, use them! Figure out a way to incorporate your strengths into your position. Some of the positions I've had weren't closely aligned to my area of passion – at first glance. However, by being creative and resourceful, I figured out a way to incorporate my areas of strength and passion into my position and day-to-day work environment.

> "I am - just as you are - a unique, never-to-be-repeated event in this universe.
>
> Therefore, I have - just as you have – a unique, never-to-be-repeated role in this world."
>
> **–GEORGE SHEEHAN**

What do you want inside and outside of your profession? What would life be like if you went to work each day and loved your job? It wasn't that long ago that I was longing for something different than being an administrative assistant. I was negative and focusing on everything about my position that I didn't like. One day, I got creative and imagined a job posting for my dream job. I had a huge epiphany when I realized most of what I imagined was exactly what I had! It was a complete shift in my thinking. My position gave me the opportunity to mentor, advise, train, speak, write, and tap into my creative and resourceful abilities, plus so much more!

# Where is your passion?

Choose to focus on what you love about your position. There are likely elements you dearly love or you wouldn't be in the position you are in. If you find you have a few sprinkles of things you love but feel you need more, find a way to make it happen. It could be as simple as the way you do your work. Perhaps you need to restructure the way you do tasks that you consider boring to make them more interesting. You may have an aptitude for writing and could partner with the person who is doing the majority of writing for your manager to begin incorporating elements of this into your position. You may have an interest and propensity in event planning, SharePoint development, website management or graphic design. Whatever your interests and strengths, you can likely partner with someone, learn and weave these elements into your day-to-day world.

Our enthusiasm and energy are high when we have passion about something. You can hear passion in people's voices and see passion in their eyes when they are talking about their passion. Passion creates energy and excitement. Are you passionate about your career? If not, what are you passionate about?

One of the reasons I wrote this book is because of my passion about the administrative profession. It is my desire to raise awareness and increase the understanding of the administrative profession to those not in the profession. It is also my desire to help administrative assistants be positive role models of our profession by utilizing the information I've shared in this book, by lifting each other up, by championing each other's successes, and by respecting our careers.

Speaking, training, mentoring, and helping others are my passions. It is what keeps me going. When I'm tired and hit one road block after another, all I have to do is think about someone who needed my experience and encouragement, or think of a younger version of myself, and realize we all need someone to coach us, empower us, pull us forward, and show us the way. Be that someone. Know you've made a difference through helping someone else.

## What will be your legacy?

If you were gone tomorrow, what would people say about you? Where have you left a memorable mark? Where have you made a difference in the life of another? What does your reputation say about you? How do people describe you?

Some of the best questions I've ever been asked are: "How do you want to feel when you go to bed and lay your head on your pillow? How do you want to feel when you wake up? How do you want to feel right now?"

Those simple questions create so many thoughts and emotions. Your answers could center you on what's really important for you. When you can lay your head on your pillow each night and quickly give thanks for all you have and all you experience, you will awaken feeling more grateful for each new day and be excited to live another day loving others and accomplishing your dreams!

I encourage you to dream. Dream big! This is what makes life exciting. Believe those dreams inside of you were planted there for a reason. Believe you can do it. Then, be bold and take action to make your dreams a reality. You are not JUST an admin. You advise and manage your manager. You are a relationship manager. You demonstrate influence and leadership. You are a trusted confidant. You are respected and valued.

## You are an Administrative Professional!

"Every memorable act in the history of the world
is a triumph of enthusiasm.

Nothing great was ever achieved without it because
it gives any challenge or any occupation, no matter
how frightening or difficult, a new meaning.

Without enthusiasm you are doomed to a life of
mediocrity but with it you can accomplish miracles."

**–OG MANDINO**

CPSIA information can be obtained
at www.ICGtesting.com
Printed in the USA
BVHW011143180419
545914BV00006B/47/P